MW00709441

HARDPRESS.NET
HOME OF HARD-TO-FIND BOOKS

The Works of William Hogarth
by Thomas Clerk

Address:
HardPress
8345 NW 66TH ST #2561
MIAMI FL 33166-2626
USA
Email: info@hardpress.net

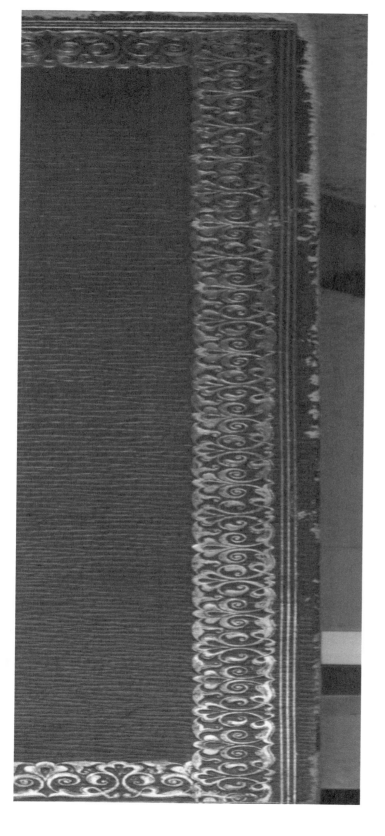

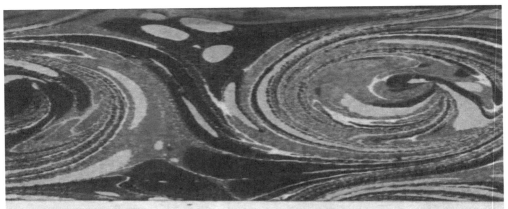

VE RI
TAS

EX·LIBRIS

THE
HARVARD UNION
FROM·THE·CLASS·OF
1 8 7 8

THE Works OF Wm Hogarth

Vol. II.

NATURE.

London Published as the Act directs by Robt Scholey 46 Paternoster Row.

THE

WORKS

OF

𝕼𝖚𝖎𝖑𝖑𝖎𝖆𝖒 𝕳𝖔𝖌𝖆𝖗𝖙𝖍,

(*INCLUDING THE 'ANALYSIS OF BEAUTY,'*)

ELUCIDATED

BY DESCRIPTIONS, CRITICAL, MORAL, AND HISTORICAL;

(FOUNDED ON THE MOST APPROVED AUTHORITIES.)

TO WHICH IS PREFIXED

SOME ACCOUNT OF HIS LIFE.

BY THOMAS CLERK.

IN TWO VOLUMES.

VOL. II.

LONDON:

PRINTED FOR R. SCHOLEY, 46, PATERNOSTER ROW;
By James Ballantyne and Co. Edinburgh.

1812.

CONTENTS

OF THE

SECOND VOLUME.

CONTENTS.

Hogarth del.

London Published as the Act directs by Robert Scholey, 46 Paternoster Row

T. Clerk sculpt

STROLLING PLAYERS,

DRESSING IN A BARN.

To those who are delighted with a diversity of contrasted figures, the present piece offers a fund of peculiar amusement. None perhaps can be filled with objects more strongly contrasted; every group is filled with humour, every subject affords food for laughter. Here we see *confusion* blended with *uniformity*, and *inconsistency* united with *propriety*; *royalty* degraded by the ensigns of *beggary*, and beggary decorated by the regalia of royalty. This print was designed by Hogarth in order to perpetuate the memory of the ridiculous shifts resorted to by strolling players just after the act was passed which prohibited their *vagabond* performances.

For wit and imagination, without any other end, Lord Orford is of opinion that this print ought to be considered as the best of all Hogarth's Works. Rouquet, who has given very cursory notice only of it, says—" The Strolling Comedians are represented in a barn, amidst a ridiculous assemblage of misery and theatrical pomp, preparing to perform a tragedy."

The scene is laid in a barn, as is intimated by the corn and flail aloft, and by the hen and chickens which are at roost upon an upright *wave*. The time is evening; and the players from the theatres at London are preparing to perform a farce; which, by the play-bill on the bed, we learn is *The Devil to pay in Heaven*, to which *celestial* amusement, rope-dancing, tumbling, &c. are to be added. The characters in this farce are, *Jupiter, Juno, Diana, Flora, Night, Syren, Aurora, Eagle, Cupid*, two devils, a ghost, and attendants.

In the centre of the print we see the cloud-compelling Jove holding Cupid's bow, and directing the urchin to reach his stockings, which had been hung up to dry in the clouds. Before him stands the chaste Diana, nearly stripped, and raving in all the high-flown rant of tragedy. At her feet is the blooming *Flora*, greasing her hair with a tallow candle, previously to powdering it with flour from a drudging-box; this goddess of the vernal flowers is so intently occupied, as not to observe that her wicker toilet has taken fire from a contiguous flame. Next her is the *ruddy Aurora*, ridding the *intoxicated Syren* of some close companions, while the latter is offering a glass of spirits to one of the company, who gladly accepts the cordial in the hope of obtaining relief from an aching tooth. At the feet of this professor of the buskin is a girl, who personates the eagle of Jove, feeding an infant with pap. Hogarth has whimsically set the sauce-pan containing the child's food upon the act against strolling players, which lies upon a crown.

At the back of this plate two young devils, whose horns are just budded, are struggling for a draught of beer: thirst and impatience are strongly marked in their eyes. Behind them a female tumbler and a veteran (whom some have conjectured to be a ghost, and others the tragic muse) are diligently occupied in cutting off a cat's tail, in order to extract the blood for some *sanguinary* transaction. Grimalkin avenges herself upon the tumbler, whose neck and face she scratches with her talons. The faces of. these two women are finely contrasted.

Below these we behold the goddess Juno, rehearsing her part, with majestic dignity; while the sable goddess NIGHT (personified by a *negro girl*) is sedulously darning a hole in one of her celestial majesty's stockings! Her reading desk is an inverted trunk, which will serve alike for the coffin of Juliet, or the concealment of Iachimo; and upon this lie a salt-box and roller, (two valuable musical instruments,) the forked thunders of Jove, and a tinder-box.

Notwithstanding all the "pomp and circumstance" with which these personages are about to make their appearance, it is obvious that they are miserably poor, having but one room for *every purpose.* This has enabled our humorous artist to group together all the concomitants of the theatre in a masterly manner. Here, then, we may see the festooned Grecian entrance, the 'curling' wave, the 'spirit stirring drum,' the furious dragon, crowns, mitres, targets, ropes, contrivances for conjuring, daggers, bowls, poison, thunder, lightning, culinary utensils, candles, and clay, and a long series of et cetera all *huddled* together;

* Works, vol. III. 456.

yet at the same time so *distinctly* are the different objects marked, that the *patient* inspector may without difficulty succeed in tracing *each*.

Although the company are obliged to employ candles, in order to prepare for their appearance, it is evidently *day light :* for, through a hole in the roof, we may discern the head of a fellow, who has clambered up to the top of the barn, and is profanely scrutinizing the mysteries of the dressing-room, unobserved by the initiated.

Mr Ireland relates, that the original picture was first sold to Francis Beckford, Esq. for *twenty-six guineas ;* by whom it was afterwards returned for the same sum; and that it was afterwards purchased for a similar sum by Mr Wood, of Littleton, in whose possession it now remains.

MOSES

BROUGHT BEFORE

PHARAOH'S DAUGHTER.

MOTTO.

Exodus, Chapter ii. *Verse* 10.

" And the child grew, and she brought him unto Pharaoh's
daughter, and he became her son ; and she called his name Moses."

THIS is an engraving from a picture belonging to
that excellent institution, the *Foundling Hospital,* to
which Hogarth was an early and liberal benefactor :
and, when the object of that noble asylum for deserted infancy is considered, it will (we think) be allowed,
that Hogarth could not have selected a more appropriate subject for his pencil.

The history of Moses, whose mother was compelled
to expose him by the cruel law of a sanguinary tyrant,
is doubtless so familiar to our readers, that it were
unnecessary to detail the particulars. The point of
time (it may be observed) is that, when the mother,
(whom the princess of Egypt had hired to " nurse
the child for her,") having brought the boy to his
protectress, is in the act of receiving her salary.
Though the daughter of Pharaoh invites and encou-

rages her adopted child, the lad fondly clings to his mother-nurse.

We must not omit to notice the attendants behind, whose manner and attitude seem to intimate a suspicion, that the infant is more nearly related to their royal mistress than she is disposed to admit. There is however a strong similarity of countenance between the boy and his patroness.

The characters of the different personages here introduced are distinctly marked and well supported. The ornaments and distant scenery are appropriate; and the crocodile creeping from beneath the princess's chair fixes the vicinity of the place to the Nile. The line of beauty on the base of the pillar is properly introduced, the Greeks being indebted to the Egyptians for their first principles of the art.

FOUR PRINTS

OF

AN ELECTION.

PLATE I.

AN ELECTION ENTERTAINMENT.

THE confusion and extravagance which not unfrequently present themselves at county elections, have afforded abundant materials for the exercise of Hogarth's comic pencil; and although the *treating act* (as it is termed) prohibits election entertainments, yet, as a record of what *was* formerly practised on such occasions, this print is abundantly deserving of attention.

Our artist then commences very properly with a dinner, which is given at an inn in a country town, agreeably to the immemorial custom of *John Bull*, who transacts no important affairs without previously taking a *hearty dinner*.

At the lower end of the table, on the right hand of the print, we see the candidate listening with all possible attention to a fat *lady*, who in her hand (which is behind him) holds a letter directed to *Sir Commodity Taxem*. The politic knight (who is said to be the late Thomas Potter, Esq.) has clasped the fair nymph with one arm ; while a girl, having fallen in love with his diamond ring, is endeavouring to detach it from his finger.   At the same time, a wag standing on a chair above him, has availed himself of the boundless familiarity (or rather licentiousness) which an election is supposed to sanction : with one hand he strikes the candidate's head against that of the woman, and *powders* his hair with the ashes of his tobacco-pipe.   Before this group is *Abel Squat*, (whose name and appearance singularly correspond,) a dealer in ribbons, gloves, and stockings, purchased as presents for the occasion ; and for which he has received a fifty pound promissory note, payable in six months : he is contemplating the paper with symptoms that do not indicate much satisfaction at his bargain.

To the left of the candidate, beneath the *Standard of Liberty and Loyalty*, another group of figures is presented : it consists of a maudlin sort of gentleman, whose arm a professor of the razor is pinching with one hand, while (resting the other on his shoulder) he *whiffs* the hot fumes of mundungus into his eyes from a short pipe. The sufferings of this friend of the candidate do not however terminate *here :* a son of St Crispin gives his right hand a friendly squeeze, that seems almost to crush every joint.

Above them are a barrister, a young woman of a pleasing countenance, and an officer paying his addresses to her, while the intoxicated lawyer flourishes a bumper over her head, and vociferates a silly toast. Next to this group, a reverend divine has divested himself of his wig, and is wiping the fumes from his head. Though the dishes are removed from table, we see the voracious divine warming the last fragments of the haunch over a chafing-dish, in order that he may devour them with the more exquisite relish.

Behind, the band of musicians is placed: it consists of a performer on the bag-pipes, who accompanies his dulcet notes with a hearty scratching;— a female professor of the violin, whose grinning countenance is expressive of the pleasure she takes in the spectacle;—and of a pompous performer on the bass viol. The notes produced by this *trio* cannot but be gratifying to the musical ears of their auditors. In the middle of the table is a crooked figure ridiculing the enormous length of *chin* possessed by the professor of the bass viol, not considering his own *deformity* in that identical part of his person.

Two of the company beneath the window appear greatly delighted with hearing the song of " *An old woman clothed in grey,*" which a droll genius * is chanting: in order to give the ballad its full effect, he has twisted a handkerchief or napkin into the representation of a face, which bears some resemblance to the gouty gentleman next him; and moves it in .conformity to that humorous song. In the mean time a waiter behind pours the contents of a vessel

---

* This is a portrait of Mr Parnell, an Irish gentleman, who was by profession an attorney, and was celebrated for his drollery and humour.

from the window upon the mob, (of the opposite party below,) who return the liquid compliment by a volley of stones, which is retorted by a man at the opposite corner, who hurls from the window a three-legged stool among the assailants.

But neither the strains of harmony nor the other discordant sounds can arouse the magistrate, whom we see expiring. He has *gorged* his stomach with oysters till he can no longer breathe; yet, true to *his* cause, even in the article of death, he grasps a fork on which an oyster is impaled. The village barber-surgeon in vain tries to *breathe a vein:* the vital spark is extinguished; and all the skill of this professor of shaving and phlebotomy is insufficient to make the purple current flow again.

Behind his worship's chair, an agent of the candidate's attempts to bribe a puritanic tailor; who, regardless of the menaces of his termagant wife, lifts up his eyes and clasped hands, and with detestation refuses the unhallowed gold. A furious scene takes place at the door. A detachment of bludgeon-men (from the adverse party) ineffectually endeavours to force a passage into the apartment.

On a chair below the defunct magistrate, a luckless wight of the law, while in the act of reckoning up the *sure and doubtful votes,* is struck in the forehead with one of the stones cast into the room by the opposite party without; he has lost his centre of gravity, and is falling prostrate to the floor. A compassionate butcher is pouring gin into a wound which a *bludgeon-man* has also received on his head from a similar missile weapon; it does not however seem to have made much impression upon the hero, who applies a glass of spirit-stirring liquor to his lips. To crown the whole, a boy is making punch in a *mashing-tub*.

The decorations of the room are suitable to the occasion. Against the wainscot are the electors' arms, viz. a CHEVRON *sable, between three guineas proper*, with an open mouth by way of crest, and the motto, " SPEAK AND HAVE." The countenances of the numerous characters here introduced are strongly marked, and well supported throughout. The face and air of the knight (Mr Ireland remarks) is perfectly of Lord Chesterfield's school ; the fellow scattering ashes on his head, and the cobler at the table, are marked with mischief. The fat woman, whom the candidate is saluting, " is of Mother Coles' family ; and the divine has the corpulence and consequence of a bishop. The two country fellows looking with delighted eyes at Mr Parnell, and an old man tortured by the gout, are admirably discriminated. The barber-surgeon and his brother butcher have so much *sang froid*, and display so little feeling for their suffering patients, that we may naturally infer each of them is in great practice." *

* Ireland's Hogarth, vol. II. p. 112.

PLATE II.

CANVASSING FOR VOTES.

FROM an election entertainment to a canvass for votes the transition is natural. We are accordingly introduced to an active canvass by the opposite party. The scene is a country village. In the centre of the print a country freeholder is beset by two inn-keepers, who solicit his vote and interest: both are offering bribes, but one is much larger than the other; and honest Hodge's *determination* may pretty easily be guessed by the cast of his eye, which significantly intimates, that though necessity obliges him to accept a *douceur* from BOTH, conscience bids him vote for the most liberal paymaster.

One of the candidates is conciliating the interest of two belles in a balcony, by purchasing a variety of trinkets from a Jew pedlar. During this transaction a porter delivers to our candidate a letter on his bended knee: he has also brought a quantity of printed bills to be distributed, which announce that Punch's theatre is opened, and invite the worthy electors to behold his performances.

The shew cloth of this exhibition is allusive to the subject. The lower part represents Punch, profusely throwing money amongst the populace; while the upper part offers a view of the Treasury, where a

ey
eag
an
sen
of t
atio
so n
A
eati
men
erci
devo
of be
two
are b
natio
piece
Th
semb
ig th
by th

waggon is in the act of being loaded with money, in order to secure parliamentary interest. In this piece Hogarth has seized the opportunity of ridiculing the clumsy and tasteless building of the Horse-guards; the arch of which is so low, that the sovereign's state-coachman, literally, cannot pass with his hat on; the turret also at the top is so low as to bear considerable resemblance to a porter-butt! The inscription to this shew-cloth is appropriate enough :— " PUNCH, CANDIDATE for GUZZLE-DOWN !"

The woman in the corner, whom the grenadier eyes so wistfully, is the mistress of the inn : she is eagerly counting her money, seated on the head of an old ship that is placed at the door; this represents a lion ready to devour a *fleur de lis*, (the arms of the old French monarchy,) and is no bad representation of that spirit of animosity which has now for so many centuries characterised the two nations.

As this scene would be imperfect without *some* eating and drinking, our artist has introduced two men in the larder, very actively occupied in the exercise of their digestive organs ; one is voraciously devouring a fowl, while the other attacks a buttock of beef. On the opposite (the left) side of the plate, two ale-house politicians—a barber and a cobler,—are busily engaged in settling the concerns of the nation, and planning sieges with half-pence and pieces of tobacco-pipe.

The back ground presents an English mob, assembled together for the patriotic purpose of breaking the windows and demolishing the house opened by the contrary party. One of this party is mounted on the cross-beam that supports the sign, and is skewering it through, forgetting that with it he also must be precipitated to the ground : in aid of his *patriotic* exertions, two fellows are with all their strength pulling a rope tied round the beam ; and so resolute are these assailants in their determinations, that they persist in their mischievous design, regardless of the blunderbuss which the enraged landlord discharges at them.

The several characters are finely discriminated.

PLATE III.

THE POLLING.

ALL the necessary preliminaries being duly adjusted, the important day for polling arrives; and we are now to contemplate both parties at the hustings, availing themselves of every possible experiment in order to swell the number of votes. The sick, the blind, the lame, the deaf, all are pressed into service on this occasion.

The rival candidates are seated on two chairs at the back of the booth, (on the right of the plate): one of them seems pretty well assured of his success, and is sitting perfectly at his ease, and resting upon his cane ; while the countenance of his opponent is marked by all that anxiety which we may suppose to agitate the mind of a candidate, with the prospect of *failure* before him. We proceed to the parties tendering their votes.

The tory interest, in order to support their pretensions, have called forth a maimed officer, who has lost a hand, an arm, and a leg in behalf of his country. The veteran, laying his *stump* upon the book, the poll (or swearing) clerk bursts into a fit of laughter ; which he endeavours to stifle with his hand, and which is not a little increased by the two barristers disputing the validity of his oath. The statute, it should be observed, required the *right* HAND (not a *stump*) to be laid upon the book, and furnishes abundant exercise to the quibbling talents of these professional gentry.

On the other side, the whigs have brought a paralytic *deaf idiot ;* he is attended by a man in fetters, who instructs him by a whisper how he must give his vote. By the shackle on this man's right leg, and the paper in his pocket, (which is entitled " *The Sixth Letter to the People of England,*") we ascertain him to be Dr *Shebbeare,* of turbulent memory ; and that he came into disgrace for being the author of that publication.* Behind him is another freeholder, brought (almost dying) from his bed. So severe is the contest, that the opposition are reduced to the necessity of procuring votes, even at the risk of life.

The squibs, &c. usually incident to elections, are not wanting here. At the extremity of the hustings a woman is *chanting* a goodly ballad, the head-piece of which is a *gibbet*, (emblematic of its contents,) which the populace below regard with much glee and attention. Amid the numerous little strokes of humour which might be pointed out, we must not omit

---

* The doctor is said to have frequently asserted in a coffee-house, that he *would* have either a pillory or a pension. He was *indulged* with both. In 1759 his " *Seventh Letter to the People of England* " exposed him to the resentment of the government ; he was *pilloried*, and imprisoned for two years. On the accession of his present majesty, he laid aside his hostility to the existing government, together with his attachment to the Stuart family, and received a pension from Lord Bute. He testified his *gratitude* by publishing several pamphlets on *the side* of government, especially at the commencement of the American war.

to notice the fellow who is sketching the countenance of the (apparently) unsuccessful candidate.

In the left-hand corner, adverting to the disgraceful scenes of *venal corruption* that *formerly* attended elections, Hogarth has introduced the chariot of Britannia breaking down, and *her* life in danger, while the coachman and footman are playing at cards upon the box, regardless of the shrieks of their mistress. Although (Lord Orford remarks) Hogarth was not happy in the introduction of this allegoric personage, yet it must be admitted that it is an admirable stroke at the interested motives of venal statesmen, who regard their own personal advantage rather than the promotion of their country's true interests. On the bridge, in the back-ground, we discern a carriage with colours flying, and a *host* of freeholders proceeding to the hustings, in order to give their *free* and *independent* votes.

PLATE IV.

CHAIRING THE MEMBER.

At length the poll is closed, and the successful candidate, seated in an arm-chair, borne by four lusty men, is here performing his triumphant *tour* round the principal streets of the borough for which he is returned to parliament. As usual in these cases, he is surrounded both by friends and foes, who mutually express their regards, not indeed in the most orderly manner.

A thresher defending his pigs, brandishes his flail at a sailor, which, in its tremendous whirl, comes in contact with the skull of one of the bearers. He reels,—he staggers at such an unexpected salute; and the person of the *member* is in imminent danger of being precipitated to his mother earth. His hat is taking an aerial flight, in which his tye-wig seems likely also to participate. Alarmed at his perilous situation, a lady in the church-yard faints away in her servants' arms : in the mean time, two urchin sweeps divert themselves by placing a pair of gingerbread spectacles upon a death's head, which appears on the gate-post. To increase the confusion, while the bear is devouring some offal, the monkey, seated on his back, has a carbine by his side, which accidentally

10

goes off, and kills the sweep upon the wall.* The ancient *fiddler* seems determined to enjoy his own music, not knowing which of the two parties is most deserving of *his* suffrage.

In the opposite corner, a soldier is regaling himself with a cheekful of the best Virginia, and preparing to dress himself after a pugilistic contest. Close by, three different cooks are conveying as many covers to the lawyer's house; in the first floor of which a company of the Tory party are recreating themselves with beholding the noise and confusion below. One of these personages (who is distinguished by a ribbon) is said to be designed for the late Duke of Newcastle, who was unusually busy at elections, in order to establish an interest by making court to the lowest of the people.

Fighting and drinking being the ordinary concomitants of such festive occasions as that now before us, Hogarth has introduced some correspondent figures. We see in the back-ground two fellows forcing their way through the crowd, with two barrels of home-brewed ale; and, close by them, a woman is inflicting condign punishment on her husband for

---

* This has been supposed to allude to the following circumstance, which took place during the Oxfordshire Election, in 1754. At the conclusion of the scrutiny, the gentlemen of the *new interest* (as they were called) set out on a grand cavalcade down the High-street. On Magdalen Bridge, some dirt and stones being thrown by the populace of the other party, a pistol was discharged from a postchaise, and shot a chimney-sweeper who was active in the assault. *Gent. Mag. vol. xxiv. p.* 289.

leaving his business : by the thread round his neck, and the scissors by his side, we ascertain that he is a tailor. Our artist (it has been remarked) seems to have had a peculiar antipathy to persons of this trade. In Le Brun's celebrated picture of the ‘ *Battle of the Granicus*,’ the painter has represented an eagle hovering over Alexander's helmet, and this idea our artist has whimsically parodied by delineating a goose fluttering over the tye-wig of the trembling candidate.

“ The ruined house,” (Mr Nichols has appropriately remarked,) “ adjoining to the attorney's, is a stroke of satire that should not be overlooked ; because it intimates that nothing can thrive in the neighbourhood of such *vermin*.”*—It was, however, more probably destroyed by a riotous mob, as having belonged to one of the adverse party.

Although, in the present scene, we see only one member *actually* chaired, yet, from the shadow against the town-hall, we may infer that the procession of the other successful candidate is just setting out. Against the church is a sun-dial, with the motto— WE MUST, beneath it, intimating that *we must die— all*. This, it must be confessed, is but a poor pun, but it is probable that Hogarth intended it so to be understood.

All the incidents in this plate are whimsically, yet skilfully combined, and with a strict regard to nature. The arch roguery of the sweeps on the wall, —the *pallid* fear imprinted on the countenance of

* Nichols's Hogarth, vol. i.

the member,—the self-complacency of the scraper on cat-gut,—the meagre French cook, and the other two English cooks, are all replete with humour, and are in every point of view most strikingly characteristic.

BEER STREET AND GIN LANE.

WE have already had occasion to remark the attention which Hogarth has paid to the selection of such subjects for many of his pictures as were calculated to instruct, while they delighted the eye of the observer. The design of this print, and of its companion piece, (Gin Lane,) is thus stated by the artist himself:

"When these two prints were designed and engraved, the dreadful consequences of gin-drinking appeared in every street. In Gin Lane every circumstance of its horrid effects is brought to view, *in terrorem.* Idleness, poverty, misery, and distress, which drives even to madness and death, are the only objects to be seen; and not a house in a tolerable condition but the pawnbroker's and gin shop.

"Beer Street, its companion, was given as a contrast, where that invigorating liquor is recommended, in order to drive the other out of vogue. Here all is joyous and thriving. Industry and jollity go hand in hand. In this happy place the pawnbroker's is the only house going to ruin; and even the small quantity of porter that he can procure is taken in at the wicket, for fear of farther distress."*

These two plates were published in the year 1751.

* Ireland's Hogarth, vol. iii. 345.

BEER STREET.

London, Published as the Act directs by Robert Scholey 46 Paternoster Row

BEER STREET.

MOTTO.

" Beer, happy produce of our isle,
Can sinewy strength impart ;
  And, wearied with fatigue and toil,
Can cheer each manly heart.

" Labour and art, upheld by thee,
Successfully advance ;
  We quaff the balmy juice with glee,
And water leave to France.

" Genius of health! thy grateful taste
Rivals the cup of Jove :
  And warms each English generous breast
With liberty and love."

In this print Hogarth offers to our view an excellent representation of John Bull in his happiest moments. A general cessation from work appears to have taken place, and all parties are regaling themselves with refreshing draughts of the cheering liquor, PORTER,— not that deleterious mixture which rumour asserts to have been imposed a few years since on the lower classes,—but the wholesome beverage, brewed from genuine malt and hops, which is calculated at once to nourish and to strengthen the honest labourer.

On the left, we have a group of jovial tap-house politicians, consisting of a butcher, a cooper, or blacksmith, (for the *trade* of this personage has not yet been ascertained by the illustrators of our artist,) and a drayman. The two former grasp a foaming pot of porter; and the cooper or blacksmith having just bought a shoulder of mutton, is waving it in the air. In the *first* stage of this print Hogarth had represented this man as elevating an astonished Frenchman from the ground *with one hand:* but the idea being rather too extravagant, he afterwards altered the engraving as it now stands. By the (late) king's speech,* and the *Daily Advertiser* lying on the table before them, it is evident they have been studying and arranging the affairs of the nation. The drayman (the last of this trio) is whispering a soft tale to the servant girl, round whose waist he has thrown one arm, while the other grasps a foaming tankard. The simplicity of the girl, in listening to this fellow's addresses, excites the risible faculties of the butcher, who indulges himself in hearty laughter at her expence.

On the right, a city porter has just set down his load of books, consigned for waste paper to Mr Pastem the trunk-maker, in St Paul's Church-yard, and

---

* The speech of his late Majesty, GEORGE II., contains the following (among other) passages, which were much admired at the time they were published—" *Let me earnestly recommend to you the advancement of our commerce and cultivating the arts of peace, in which you may depend on my hearty concurrence and encouragement.*"

is about to recruit his spirits by an invigorating draught. Two fishwomen in the centre are supplied with a flaggon of beer, and are singing with much glee Mr Lockman's verses on the herring fishery.* Behind, some paviours are refreshing themselves while at work; and still further in the back-ground, two chairmen have set down their massy load, (a dame of quality going to court,) and are in like manner resting their exhausted strength and spirits.

In a garret window we see three journeymen tailors, and, on the roof of the adjoining house, several bricklayers, all partaking of the general hilarity. This next house belongs to a publican, whom, by his repairing it, we may reasonably infer to be in the high 'way to wealth;' while the pawnbroker's dwelling opposite, is fast verging to decay for want of trade.

The meagre, lank-visaged artist, who is copying a bottle from one hanging before him, has been considered as a satire on John Stephen Liotard, a portrait painter and enameller, who came from Geneva in the reign of George II., and of whom Lord Orford has left the following character:

" Devoid of imagination, and, one would think, of memory, he could render nothing but what he saw before his eyes; freckles, marks of the small-pox,

* At the time these prints were published, British herrings became very plentiful, under the protection of the society for promoting the British fisheries. To this society Mr Lockman was secretary: the ballad in question, which he wrote on the herring fishery, was set to music, and sung with very great applause at Vauxhall.

every thing found its place; not so much from fide-lity, as because he could not conceive the absence of any thing that appeared to him. Truth prevailed in all his works, grace in very few or none." *

* Works, vol. iii. 474.

fide-
ce of
:d in

London Published as the act directs by Wᵐ Hogarth Septembᵉʳ 1751

GIN LANE.

MOTTO.

" Gin, cursed fiend, with fury fraught,
Makes human race a prey;
  It enters by a deadly draught,
And steals our life away.

  " Virtue and truth, driv'n to despair,
Its rage compels to fly;
  But cherishes, with hellish care,
Theft—murder—perjury.

  " Damn'd cup! that on the vitals preys,
That liquid fire contains,
  Which madness to the heart conveys,
And rolls it through the veins."

THE last scene presented us with a faithful delineation of health, content, and good humour: we have now to contemplate the hideous contrast, produced by the general use of British spirits among the poor. In *Beer Street*, it may be recollected, that all the houses (*the pawnbroker's only excepted*) were in good repair. In *Gin Lane*, Master GRIPE's alone (beside the dwellings of the distiller and undertaker) is in good condition, nearly all the others being in a tottering, ruinous state. This miscreant's name and business admirably correspond. Behold him (on the right of the plate) *scrutinizing* the tendered articles by way of pledge, lest he should lend too much upon them. One of his customers is a journeyman carpenter, pawning his *saw;* while a tattered female brings her tea-kettle and other articles, in order to obtain the means of purchasing the deleterious (may we be permitted to add *infernal*) spirit, which has—vulgarly indeed—but most emphatically, been termed STRIP ME NAKED!

Opposite the pawnbroker's door, against the wall, are two figures stupefied by the noxious draught; one of them (a woman) has fallen asleep, and thereby gives the snail—fit emblem of sloth—an opportunity of creeping over her. The other, a boy, tormented with famine, which is indelibly impressed on his countenance, is gnawing a bare bone, the possession of which a hungry bull-dog is contesting with him.

At the top of the steps a more disgusting object presents itself.——An intoxicated mother (whose legs are broken out into ulcers) is taking snuff, regardless of her infant, which falls into the area of a gin cellar. Over the entrance to this cavern of despair, an inscription was engraved on the larger plates, but which would not have been legible in our copies, if we had attempted to have introduced them: it is however too horribly appropriate to be omitted, and runs as follows :——" DRUNK FOR A PENNY : DEAD DRUNK FOR TWO-PENCE : CLEAN STRAW FOR NOTHING."

At the foot of the steps, a retail vender of gin and ballads is at the point of expiring ; *corroded* by the constant use of that ardent spirit, we see him reduced to a skeleton, after having pawned or bartered his shirt, waistcoat, and stockings. The scene in the back-ground is not less disgusting.

Among the various figures introduced, we see an old woman in the act of being conveyed to her lodgings in a wheelbarrow, followed by a young fellow, who tenders an additional glass to her. In the garret above, a barber has in a fit of insanity hung himself; beneath, is a crowd assembled at the door of Killman the distiller, anxiously expecting their respective allowances. Among them, we contemplate a mother drenching her infant with *the liquid-fire;* while two charity girls are mutually drinking healths in the same detestable beverage; and still further back, two (*apparently*) lame beggars are quarrelling,—one of whom wields his crutch with much dexterity, while his antagonist levels a stool at his devoted head.

Two more objects remain to be noticed. The one is a beautiful female, killed by the excessive use of this ardent spirit, whose corpse two men are placing in a shell by order of the parish beadle. The officer's compassionate attention seems to be directed to her orphan child, who is loudly lamenting for the loss of its mother. The other object is a dancing maniac, " grinning horribly a ghastly smile," with a pair of bellows in one hand, and his child impaled on a spit in the other. The agonized mother is screaming behind him. But we forbear to expatiate on a subject so detestably horrid as this part of the present plate.

The scene is laid in St Giles's parish, the lower inhabitants of which, in Hogarth's time, were notorious for their immorality and depravity: although circumstances have somewhat changed the *face* of things, still that part of the metropolis calls aloud for the intervention of some friendly power. And the *curious* observer of manners, who is disposed to risk his person, may, in some parts, still behold the pewter measures chained to the tables of the liquor houses, and hear the chains clanked, in order that the empty vessels may be replenished.

l-
h,
e
is
r-
l-
d
y

THE INVASION;

OR,

ENGLAND AND FRANCE.

PLATE I.

ENGLAND.

MOTTO.

" See John the soldier, Jack the tar,
With sword and pistol arm'd for war,
    Should *Mounseer* dare come here :
The hungry slaves have smelt our food,
They long to taste our flesh and blood,
    Old England's beef and beer !

" Britons, to arms ! and let 'em come,
Be you but Britons still,——strike home !
    And lion-like attack 'em !
No power can stand the deadly stroke
That's given from hands and hearts of oak,
    With liberty to back 'em."

THIS print and its companion were published in the
year 1756, when a war broke out between this country

and France. The present scene is designed to shew the alacrity of all parties in coming forward on that occasion, in order to support their country's interest.

In the group on the right, a gallant peasant relinquishes the guidance of the plough, to wield a musket; and lest his being *under the standard* should cause his rejection, he is deceiving the serjeant by standing on tip-toe.

On the opposite side, a grenadier is chalking on the wall of the public house a figure of his majesty of France, whose robe is covered with fleurs-de-lis; and, agreeable to the custom of that day, a label is appended to his mouth with the following sentences: —" *You take a' my fine ships; you be de pirate; you be de teef; me send my grand armies and hang you all.*" Correspondent with this threat, the *grand monarque* grasps in one hand a gibbet, and lays the other on his sword.

This circumstance excites the mirth of the soldier and sailor, who, with their girls, are standing by, and seem greatly to enjoy this *chef d'œuvre* of art. One of the latter places her forefinger against the prongs of a *fork*, to shew (Mr Ireland observes) that the performance has *some point*, while the other measures the capacious breadth of the military artist's shoulders.

The scene is laid at the sign of the late gallant *Duke of Cumberland*, who is mounted on a proud charger: on the table out of doors a buttock of beef invites attention. The soldier has laid his sword across the latter, and the sailor has placed his pistols over a tankard of strong beer. The paper lying on the table is the celebrated national song of " *Rule*

Britannia; and the little fifer playing *God save the King,* is the same whom we have seen in the MARCH TO FINCHLEY.

The back-ground exhibits a serjeant drilling a company of young recruits.

The mirth, good humour, and air of content delineated on the countenances of the figures here introduced, presents a striking contrast to the lank and meagre personages whom we now proceed to contemplate in the companion to this print.

PLATE II.

FRANCE.

MOTTO.

" With lanthorn jaws, and croaking gut,
See how the half-starved Frenchmen strut,
  And call us English dogs ;
But soon we'll teach these bragging foes,
That beef and beer give heavier blows
  Than soup and roasted frogs.

The priests, inflamed with righteous hopes,
Prepare their axes, wheels, and ropes,
  To bend the stiff-neck'd sinner ;
But, should they sink in coming over,
Old Nick may fish 'twixt France and Dover,
  And catch a glorious dinner." *

THE scene before us represents an embarkation of
French troops, in order to invade England : so little
are the troops disposed to go on this hazardous expedition, that the serjeant is obliged to goad them
on with his halbert !

The meagre appearance of the troops is very
broadly accounted for by their unsubstantial diet.

* These verses, and those in the preceding print, were written
by Mr Garrick.

T
ho
(w
" ,
roy
boi
offi
ber
by l
the
lett
BLU
and ,
men
diers
our s

Bu
this e
much
heret
scroll
' be .
he ha
accon
and of
adding
he is t
he es

In t
culture
way a
ng up

The fore-ground of this plate exhibits a little ale-house, whose sign is a *wooden shoe*, with the inscription (which could not here be reduced so as to be legible) " *soup maigre a la sabot royal*,"—(soup meagre at the royal wooden shoe.) In the larder, such as it is, some bones of beef (void of flesh) are suspended, and an officer is in the very humble office of roasting a number of *frogs*, which he has spitted on his sword. Close by him is the royal standard of France, which has (in the larger prints) the following inscription in large letters :—VENGEANCE, AVEC LE BON BIER, ET BON BEUF, D'ANGLETERRE,"—*Vengeance, with the good beer and good beef of England*. This seems to excite a momentary joy in the countenances of some of the soldiers, who apparently are devouring by anticipation our substantial British fare.

But though the military do not in general relish this expedition, the priest before us seems to enjoy much gratification in the prospect of compelling the heretics to return into the bosom of the church. The scroll in the sledge contains a plan for a monastery *to be erected* at Blackfriars ; and in the same vehicle he has already deposited an image of St Anthony, accompanied by his pig, a gibbet, scourges, wheels, and other instruments of torture ; and is in the act of adding to them an axe, the sharpness of whose edge he is trying with his fingers. These are designed for the establishment of a British INQUISITION.

In the back-ground, in order to intimate that agriculture must suffer by the invasion having taken away all the men, two women are introduced ploughing up a barren promontory. If we may credit the

1

assertions of some recent travellers in France, the restless ambition of its present ruler furnishes such incessant employment for his *male* subjects, who are capable of bearing arms, that the agricultural labour is, in several departments, performed almost exclusively by women.

THE COUNTRY INN-YARD;

OR,

THE STAGE COACH.

The scene here presented to us is such an one as must be familiar to the recollection of every spectator who has left his tranquil home, whether for business or for pleasure. The bustle and consequence of the landlady in the bar are well contrasted by the obsequiousness of the landlord, who seems to be vouching for the moderation of every item in his bill. His asseverations do not appear to carry conviction to the mind of the paymaster. A fat lady is forcing her way into the coach, while a fellow-traveller holds her dram-bottle. Opposite to the latter, a rich old fellow (who has come part of his way in a post-chaise) disregards the application of the hump-backed postillion for the accustomed fee. The old dame in the basket behind, enjoys her pipe of Virginia with great complacency. On the roof of the vehicle are seated an English sailor and a French lacquey, whose countenances afford a good contrast of the manners of the two nations.

The noise and confusion usually incident to country inn-yards, are much increased by the noisy fellow

at the window, who is raising some dulcet notes on
his French-horn, while the landlady rings in vain for
her chambermaid, whom a fellow is kissing in the
passage. And in the back-ground an election procession is about to set out. The performers in this farce
have chaired a figure, in one of whose hands they have
placed a horn-book, and in the other a rattle. This
was intended for *Child* Lord Castlemain, (afterwards
Lord Tylney,) who opposed Sir Robert Abdy and
Mr Bramston, in a strong contest for the county of
Essex. The horn-book, bib, and rattle are obviously
allusive to the name, viz. *Child.* At the election a
man was placed on a bulk, with a figure representing
a child in his arms; and as he whipped it, he ex-
claimed—" What, *you little child,* must you be a member?" In this disputed election, it appeared from the
register book of the parish where Lord Castlemain
was born, that he was only twenty years of age when
he offered himself a candidate. The family name was
changed from Child to Tylney, by act of parliament,
in the year 1735.

Trusler thinks that the scene is at an inn on the
Dover road; but it is more likely to be somewhere
in Essex; though it has puzzled the ingenuity of
former illustrators of our artist to ascertain the particular place.

s on
i for
the
ces-
arce
iave
This
irds
and
y of
isly
)n a
:ing
ex-
em-
the
iain
hen
was
ent,

the
iere
: of
)ar-

PAUL BEFORE FELIX.

PLATE I.

MOTTO.

Acts, Chapter xxiv. *Verse 25.*

" And, as he reasoned of righteousness, temperance, and judgment to come, Felix trembled."

THE original picture is at present in Lincoln's Inn Hall, in which the Lord Chancellor holds his sittings after the several terms for dispatching the suits in the court of Chancery, which, being a court of equity, is perhaps not inappositely, decorated with a picture representing an unjust judge writhing under all the tortures of an agonized, guilty conscience. As the circumstances to which the artist alludes must be familiar to every one who peruses the sacred volume, we proceed directly to a concise examination of the print.

The proconsul Felix is surrounded by the fasces, standard, and other appendages of office. He is recorded to have been rapacious, intemperate, and unjust : with peculiar propriety, therefore, does the apostle urge righteousness and temperance, and enforce his appeal by the doctrine of a future judgment. The magistrate trembles, while the prisoner speaks with firmness; the prisoner, though in chains, makes his judge to tremble! The attention of the whole court is fixed, and their countenances indicate the thoughts that agitate their breasts. One is enraptured at his doctrine; a second receives the dreadful truths with salutary fear;—while a third is internally convicted, a fourth hangs as it were on the apostle's lips for the celestial accents. Even Tertullus (who is standing under the column on the right) ceases his accusation with disappointed amazement. The *physiognomy* of the high priest Ananias evidently declares his abhorrence of the man; and indicates, that notwithstanding he is unable to resist the convincing weight of the apostle's arguments, still he cannot conceal his professed hatred of the Christians.

Although Hogarth does not excel in historical composition, yet it must be admitted, that this picture is not altogether unworthy of his talents. The characters are all strongly marked; the attitudes are judiciously varied.

l en-
ent
eaks
akes
hole
the
ared
aths
con-
lips
o is
his
phy-
de-
that
ing
not

ical
pic-
The
are

Hogarth del.

D.P. Pariʃ sculp.

London, Published as the Act directs by Robert Scholey, 46 Paternoster Row.

PLATE II.

PAUL BEFORE FELIX.

THERE is but little difference between this plate and the last. The countenances indeed are somewhat varied, and Drusilla, the wife of Felix, is *here* introduced, agreeably to the sacred record. The artist has described her as a fine woman, whose beauty is heightened by the contrasted features of the persons around her. The presence of this woman serves to exalt the character of Paul, the subject of whose discourse before Felix is chosen with singular propriety. Drusilla was a Jewess; her fisrt husband (a heathen sovereign) submitted to the most rigorous ceremony of Judaism, in order to gratify her : but Felix, being struck with her charms, prevailed on her to leave her lawful husband and marry him. Drusilla is not the first person whom ambition, or the love of riches and honour, has prevailed upon to desert the sober path of rectitude.

This print is also from the original in Lincoln's Inn Hall, but is less known than the preceding picture on the same subject, the wife of Felix having been omitted, because the apostle's hand was improperly placed before her. Though the present plate has been held in little estimation, yet, as an undoubted production of Hogarth's pencil, it was too valuable to be omitted : we have therefore given it a place in our collection.

PLATE III.

PAUL BEFORE FELIX.

THE avowed design of this very humorous print was to ridicule Rembrandt's style of etching, which prevailed greatly at the time Hogarth flourished. The *dramatis personæ* are the same as in the two former plates. The proconsul may easily be ascertained by his laurelled brow; Drusilla (who sits next him) is delineated with a dog in her lap, in ridicule of the foolish fondness of some modern ladies for the canine race; her olfactory nerves, as well as those of her companion, appear to be violently affected. The high priest, swollen with pride and indignation, seems almost to start from his seat, and sacrifice the apostle, but that a senator prevents him; while Tertullus, arrayed as a *serjeant at law*, is rending his brief in a fit of mortified pride and revenge. The attitudes and countenances of the officers of the court, and other spectators, are correspondent with the true Dutch style, which this print was designed to satirize.

Our artist has delineated Paul as a little mean-looking man, and accordingly has placed him on a stool, in order that he may command the court. A fat unwieldy *guardian* angel lies *asleep* at his feet; of which opportunity a little imp avails himself with a malignant grin, to saw the leg of the stool asunder, and precipitate the apostle to the ground. Behind

creeps
name .
He see
tering
Abo
statue
ed : sh
impart
knife,
the ar
goddes
port th
At tl
ress is
brief;
persona
is fast
éloquer
hurt, i
senses
some n
at by
The Je
at the
The
receipt
Mos
hurry
tende
with f
ertain
som

creeps a black snarling cur, belonging to Felix, whose name appears inscribed on the collar round his neck. He seems ready to seize St Paul the moment his tottering stool gives way.

Above, on the left of the print, appears a jolly statue of JUSTICE, one only of whose eyes is covered : she stands majestically poising in one hand the *impartial* scales, while the other brandishes a *butcher's knife*, on the blade of which is engraven a dagger, (the arms of the city of London). This corpulent goddess, grown fat by the law, is scarcely able to support the massy bags of gold that hang at her side.

At the feet of Tertullus, a malicious imp of darkness is eagerly gathering up the fragments of his brief; and at the table behind him several curious personages are introduced. One of these (a woman) is fast asleep, regardless of the apostle's torrent of eloquence; the next, who is apparently the *clerk in-court*, is sagaciously mending a pen; the olfactory senses of the two next are grievously offended by some noxious odour, the cause of which is pointed out by the venerable bearded figure next the scribe. The Jew who stands next is in an attitude of amaze at the vehement action and language of Paul.

The print now described was originally given as a receipt ticket to the serious *Paul before Felix*, and to *Moses brought before Pharaoh's daughter*. The *drowsy* angel (Mr J. Ireland has been informed) was intended for Luke Sullivan, an engraver whom Hogarth frequently employed; but it is by no means certain who was the original portrait of Tertullus : by some it has been said to represent a Mr Hugh

Campbell, an advocate, *not* remarkable for much elegance of style or politeness of manners; while others assert it to have been designed for Dr W. King, formerly principal of St Mary's Hall, Oxford; and, in proof of their assertion, refer to an ascertained portrait in Worlidge's *View of Lord Westmoreland's Installation* (1761,) to which it has a striking resemblance.*

* Mr J. Ireland's Hogarth, vol. ii. p. 88.

muc
whi
Dr W.
xford.
ascer-
stmore
triking

London Published as the Act directs by Robert Scholey 46 Paternoster Row.

SLEEPING CONGREGATION.

THE scene of the present picture is laid in a country church, erected, it should seem, at a time when our ancestors paid but little regard to the lighter orders of architecture: the sombre appearance of the edifice is sufficient of itself to invite the occupiers of its pews to gentle slumber, independently of any gentle opiate which the officiating minister may supply.

The text* from which our drowsy divine is preaching, is admirably suited to the rustic audience, who, fatigued by the labour of the preceding week, have taken him at his word, and who (with the exception of two wakeful old sinners and the clerk) are all quietly taking their rest. As it was formerly the custom to place an hour-glass by the preacher's side by way of admonition, our pulpit orator is accordingly equipped with that memento of departing hours; and on the side of the pulpit the following *appropriate text* (which could not but be sufficiently reduced to be legible here) was inscribed:—" *I am afraid of you, lest I have bestowed upon you labour in vain.*"—(Gal. iv. 2.) The

* " *Come unto me all ye that labour and are heavy laden, and I will give you rest.*" (Matt. xi. 28.)

drawling manner of the parson is delineated in his countenance.

The clerk beneath is a worthy associate of such a pastor; his physiognomy is expressive of all that self-consequence which frequently marks these sapient officers of the church. It is evident that a warmer subject occupies his attention than the eloquence of the clergyman. He is wantonly gazing at a damsel who has fallen asleep while studying the office of matrimony, and who is probably dreaming of all the joys incident to wedded life. The fellows snoring below appear to be well practised performers in nasal music, and, together with the harmonious notes breathed slowly and solemnly from the nasal organs of the men in the gallery above, they unite in forming a delightful concert, in which, however, the thorough-bass seems to preponderate.

The windows of the church (though apparently designed to match) do not correspond; over them are the royal arms, the motto of which is supported by a flying angel, that more resembles one of Neptune's Tritons than a celestial messenger. The triangle, surrounded by a glory, is the manufacture of some rural mechanic, who thereby designed to convey an idea of the most sacred doctrine of Christianity, a doctrine founded indeed upon the infallible volume of inspiration, but which such clumsy representations as these are rather calculated to bring into contempt than to explain.

The soporific pastor is said (on what authority we know not) to have been designed for Dr Desaguliers.

l in hi

such i
at sel
sapien
varme
nce o
damse
tice of
all the
noring
1 nasal
notes
organs
form-
r, the

rently
them
ortec
Nep-
le tri-
ure of
) con-
hris-
alible
repre-
bring

iority
Desa-

LAUGHING AUDIENCE

London Published by the Author to be had of him at Leicester Fields

LAUGHING AUDIENCE.

A POWERFUL contrast to the preceding print is offered to our consideration in the picture now to be described. It is a representation of one of the *Theatres Royal*, and exhibits (at the bottom) one end of the orchestra,—behind, a corner of the pit, and above, part of the side boxes. Here we behold two beaux, arrayed in all the fantastic garb of the *haut ton ;* one of them is holding amorous parley with an orange girl, while the other presents his snuff-box to a lady. Notwithstanding the pit (with the exception of one stern critic only) appear convulsed with laughter, these personages have too much politeness to pay any attention to the comedy which is performing. The dress of the beaux affords no bad chronicle of the disregard entertained by our forefathers for those antiquated things called *convenience* and *consistency.*

In the laughter-loving faces in the pit, we may observe every gradation, from the prudish simper to the broad grin of boyish folly,—the smile of approbation, and the loud roar of sapient applause.

The three musicians in the orchestra are so accustomed to similar scenes, that they pay as little regard to the humour of the piece as the sage critic, whose head is covered by an enormous bushy peruke.

The Laughing Audience was published in 1733, as a *subscription ticket* to the " Rake's Progress" and " Southwark Fair."——The receipt was afterwards cut off.

COLUMBUS

BREAKING THE EGG.

THIS print also was engraved as a receipt ticket, and was, in 1752, given by Hogarth to the subscribers for his "Analysis of Beauty." Its design is to ridicule that spirit of detraction which refuses the deserved meed to real merit, and to useful discoveries.

As the history of Columbus is, in fact, the history of the discovery of the new world, (for he unquestionably first discovered the continent of America, and not Americo Vespucci,) we are of necessity restricted to a simple recital of the anecdote on which the print is founded.

In the year 1499, Columbus (who was a native of Genoa) sailed on a voyage of discovery at the expense of Ferdinand and Isabella, the sovereigns of Spain, when he first explored the continent of America. On his return home, he met with the reception which has not unfrequently been given to men of distinguished merit. The Spaniards, instead of rightly estimating the services he had rendered to them, undervalued, and even ridiculed the discoveries he had made. To convince them of the folly of such a mode of thinking and acting, at a public supper he proposed to some of these malignants to set an egg upright on its smaller end. The table was cleared, and after these bunglers had *fruitlessly* attempted it,—" We will try," said the adventurous navigator, and striking the small end of the egg smartly upon the table, it remained erect. The emotions to which this simple discovery gave existence are strongly delineated in the faces of the haughty dons. Disappointed pride is evidently stamped on the two whose fingers are applied to the eggs, in order to keep them upright; a drivelling simper appears in him who stands at Columbus's right hand; the speckled phiz of the man on his left is singularly expressive of stupid astonishment; while the proud señor behind his chair belabour: stupid head for not hitting on the right way. Columbus, however, maintains the dignity of a great mind, conscious of its superiority.

The articles on the table are introduced with great propriety : the eels twisted round the eggs are illustrative of the line of beauty explained in the *Analysis;* and which is further intimated by the curve of the knives and forks lying upon the table.

The treatment of Columbus evidently refers to that which the artist himself expected to incur from the critics, and which he in fact did receive on what he called his own discovery, and which he has illustrated in the above-mentioned treatise.

i.

sed to se
ight on a
after the
Ve w...ng
ng the s...
it remain
e discove
n the las
is evident
lled to th
t drivelng
Columb...
nan on b
punishmen
labour.
way. C
of a gr

with gre
ys are ...
ne *Analys*
irve of t

y refers
incur ing
ve on w
e has ha

PL. LXIII.

SARAH MALCOM.

London Published as the Act directs by Robert Scholey 46 Paternoster Row.

SARAH MALCOLM,

WHO WAS EXECUTED ON WEDNESDAY THE 7TH OF MARCH,
1733, FOR THE MURDER OF MRS LYDIA DUNCOMBE,
ELIZABETH HARRISON, AND ANN PRICE.

—————

THE portrait of this murderess was painted in Newgate by Hogarth, to whom she sat for her picture
two days before her execution, having previously
dressed herself for the purpose.

The circumstances attending the conviction and
execution of this woman are briefly these :

On Sunday, Feb. 4, 1733, Mrs Lydia Duncombe,
(aged 60,) and Elizabeth Harrison her companion,
were found strangled, and Ann Price (her maid, aged
17,) with her throat cut, at Mrs Duncombe's apart-
ments in Tanfield Court, in the Inner Temple. Sarah
Malcolm (who was a chare-woman) was on the same
evening apprehended on the information of Mr Kerrel, who had chambers on the same staircase, and
who had found some bloody linen under his bed, and
a silver tankard in a close-stool, which she had concealed there.*

* Our account is drawn up from a careful comparison of the
Gent. Mag. vol. iii. (for February and March, 1733,) p. 97, 99, 137,
153, with Mr J. Ireland's narrative in his Hogarth Illustrated, vol. ii.
p. 313, 321, to which we refer once for all.

On her examination before Sir Richard Brocas, she confessed to sharing in the produce of the robbery, but declared herself innocent of the murders; asserting upon oath, that Thomas and James Alexander, and Mary Tracy, were principal parties in the whole transaction. Notwithstanding this, the coroner's jury brought in their verdict of wilful murder against Sarah Malcolm only, it not then *appearing that any other person was concerned.* Her confession they considered as a mere subterfuge, none knowing such people as she pretended were her accomplices.

A few days after, a boy about seventeen years of age was hired as a servant by a person who kept the Red Lion alehouse at Bridewell Bridge; and hearing it said, in his master's house, that Sarah Malcolm had given in an information against one Thomas and James Alexander, and Mary Tracy, said to his master, " My name is James Alexander, and I have a brother named Thomas, and my mother nursed a woman where Sarah Malcolm lived." Upon this acknowledgment, the master sent to Alstone, turnkey of Newgate; and the boy being confronted with Malcolm, she immediately charged him with being concealed under Mrs Duncombe's bed, previously to letting in Tracy and his brother, by whom and himself the murders were committed. On this evidence he was detained; and frankly telling where his brother and Tracy were to be found, they also were taken into custody, and brought before Sir Richard Brocas: here Malcolm persisted in her former asseverations; but the magistrate thought her unworthy of credit, and would have discharged them, but being advised

3

by some persons present to act with more caution, committed them all to Newgate. Their distress was somewhat alleviated by the gentlemen of the Temple Society, who, fully convinced of their innocence, allowed each of them one shilling per diem during the time of their confinement. This ought to be recorded to the honour of the *law*, as it has not often been the *practice* of the profession.

Though Malcolm's presence of mind seems to have forsaken her at the time when she lurked about the Temple, without making any attempt to escape, and left the produce of her theft in situations that rendered discovery inevitable, she by the time of trial recovered her recollection, made a most acute and ingenious defence,* and cross examined the witnesses with all the black-robed artifice of a gentleman *bred up* to the bar. The circumstances were, however, so clear as to leave no doubt in the minds of the court, and the jury brought in their verdict, *guilty*.

On Wednesday the 7th of March, about ten in the morning, she was taken in a cart from Newgate to the place of execution, facing Mitre-court, Fleet-street, and there suffered death on a gibbet erected for the occasion. She was neatly dressed in a crape mourning gown, white apron, sarcenet hood, and black gloves ; carried her head aside with an air of

---

* One part of her defence was, it must be acknowledged, rather weak : she declared that seventeen pounds of the money found in her hair was sent to her by her father ; but, on inquiry, it was proved that he lived in a state of extreme and pitiable poverty in the city of Dublin, where she was born. Gent. Mag. vol. iii. p. 154.

affectation, and was said to be painted. She was attended by Dr Middleton of St Bride's, her friend Mr Peddington, and Guthrie, the ordinary of Newgate. She appeared devout and penitent, and earnestly requested Peddington would print a paper she had given him * the night before, which contained,— *not* a confession of the murder, but protestations of her innocence, and a recapitulation of what she had before said relative to the Alexanders, &c. This wretched woman, though only twenty-five years of age, was so lost to all sense of her situation, as to rush into eternity with a lie upon her lips. She much wished to see Mr Kerrel, and acquitted him of every imputation thrown out at her trial.

After she had conversed some time with the ministers, and the executioner began to do his duty, she fainted away; but recovering, was in a short space afterwards executed. Her corpse was carried to an undertaker's on Snow-Hill, where multitudes of people resorted, and gave money to see it: among the rest, a gentleman in deep mourning kissed her, and gave the attendants half-a-crown.

Professor Martin dissected this notorious murderess, and afterwards presented her skeleton, in a glass case, to the Botanic Gardens at Cambridge, where it still remains.†

---

* This paper he sold for twenty pounds! and the substance of it was printed in the Gentleman's Magazine for 1733, p. 137.

† In the Gentleman's Magazine, (for 1733, p. 154,) however, it is erroneously said that she was buried in St Sepulchre's church-yard.

Besides the present portrait, Hogarth executed a full-length of this atrocious offender ; from which it should seem probable that the artist painted her twice.   There is also a figure of her cut on wood in the Gentleman's Magazine for March, 1733, slightly differing from our engraving.

SIMON LORD LOVAT.

═══

Tʜɪs nobleman (who was executed for aiding the Pretender in the rebellion of 1745) sat for the present picture to Hogarth at St Albans, who, having formerly been acquainted with him, went thither for that purpose. He is painted in the act of counting the rebel forces with his fingers; and those who knew the Scottish peer have pronounced the portrait to be a most faithful likeness.

"Lord Lovat was one of the last chieftains that preserved the rude manners and barbarous authority of the early feudal ages. He resided in a house which would be esteemed but an indifferent one for a very private plain country gentleman in England, as it had properly only four rooms on a floor, and those not large. Here, however, he kept a sort of court, and several public tables; and a numerous body of retainers always attending. His own constant residence, and the place where he always received company, even at dinner, was the very same room where he lodged; and his lady's sole apartment was her bed-room; and the only provision for the lodging of the servants and retainers was a quantity of straw, which they spread every night on the floors of the lower rooms, where the whole inferior part of the

Hogarth del.   C. Clark sculp.

London Published as the Act directs by Robert Scholey 46 Paternoster Row.

family, consisting of a very great number of persons, took up their abode." *

From his own account, (as published in his memoirs,†) Lord Lovat seems to have been a man devoid of any fixed principle, except that of self-interest: and on his conduct during the rebellion of 1745, Sir William Young (one of the managers appointed by the house of commons for conducting the prosecution) has the following observations, which are not calculated to place his character in a very amiable point of view:

" Your lordships have already done national justice on some of the principal traitors who appeared in open arms against his majesty, by the ordinary course of law; but this noble lord, who in the whole course of his life has boasted of his superior cunning in wickedness, and his ability to commit frequent treasons with impunity, vainly imagined that he might possibly be a traitor in private, and rebel only in his heart, by sending his son and his followers to join the Pretender, and remaining at home himself, to endeavour to deceive his majesty's faithful subjects; hoping *he* might be rewarded for his son's services, if successful, or his *son* alone be the sufferer for *his* offences, if the undertaking failed. Diabolical cunning! Atrocious impiety!" ‡

* King's observations on ancient castles, inserted in vol. iv. of " Archæologia, or miscellaneous tracts relating to antiquity," &c.

† He wrote them originally in French, from which language they were translated into English and published in 8vo, 1797, though they had been printed for several years before, but withheld till that time for some private reasons.

‡ State Trials, vol. iv. p. 627.

Lord Lovat suffered the execution of his sentence with fortitude. He was beheaded by the *maiden*, (an implement of death appropriated to state criminals in North Britain,) of which the guillotine (which was so destructively employed during the French revolution) is an improvement.

This plate had a very extensive circulation; it was reduced into a small size, and engraved for a watch-paper.

ence
. (an
inals
was
·olu·

; it
or a

Pl. LIV.

TIME SMOKING A PICTURE

Hogarth del.

E.E.Pye sculp.

London Published as the Act directs by Robert Scholey 46 Paternoster Row.

Tн
tion
whic
briefl
satire

_Fa_
and s
his sci
canva
tion o
rord
stand
chara
in me
spirit
by int
script

TIME

SMOKING A PICTURE.

THIS plate, Mr Nichols informs us, was a subscription ticket for Hogarth's Sigismunda, the history of which having already been given,* it only remains briefly to describe the object of the artist's animated satire.

Father Time is here sitting on a mutilated statue, and smoking a landscape which he has pierced with his *scythe*, in order to evince its antiquity;—a damaged canvas, as well as sombre tints, being (in the estimation of some cognoscenti) infallible marks of the true *verd antique*. Beneath the easel on which it is fixed stands an ample jar of *varnish*. This is strikingly characteristic. By part of this print being executed in mezzotinto and the remainder etched, it has a spirited appearance, and the burlesque is increased by introducing the fragments with the following inscription beneath (which is found in the larger plate):

" As statues moulder into worth."—P. W.

* See vol. i. p. 14. et seq.

BEGGAR'S OPERA.

The scene of this plate is laid in the third act of Gay's very popular opera; and as the names of the principal performers of the piece here burlesqued, together with those of the audience whose portraits are introduced, are given in our engraving, little further explanation seems necessary.

The Beggar's Opera, it may be observed, was written by Gay to ridicule the absurd Italian Operas, and was originally performed at the Theatre in Lincoln's Inn Fields, in the year 1727 : so great was the applause with which it was received, that *sixty-three* successive performances were requisite to gratify the public curiosity; this success can only be paralleled by the astonishing run of Mr Sheridan's Pizarro a few years since. The Beggar's Opera continues to be occasionally performed, notwithstanding its immoral tendency; and we understand that a burletta founded upon it is in a course of performance at one of the minor theatres of the metropolis for the *edification* of the London youth.

Our great moralist Johnson, however, was of opi-

nio
to
yet
cha
ple.
of a
tru
by
deb
fact
tion
licit
pror
"
dren
their
gno
sarc
tons
OPE
"
the
think
ight
hath
sure
gen

nion, that although more influence has been ascribed to the Beggar's Opera than in reality it ever had, yet that it *might* have some influence by making the character of a rogue familiar, and in some degree pleasing. "*There is*" (says he) " such a LABEFACTION *of all principles as may be injurious to morality.*" The truth of the doctor's remark is most amply confirmed by the two following anecdotes, for which we are indebted to Mr Ireland, under whose observance the facts took place. We think they must carry conviction to every unprejudiced mind, and too much publicity cannot be given to whatever is calculated to promote the moral benefit of society.

" Two boys, under nineteen years of age, children of worthy and respectable parents, fled from their friends, and pursued courses that threatened an ignominious termination to their lives. *After much search, they were found engaged in midnight depredations, and in each of their pockets was the* BEGGAR'S OPERA."

" A boy of seventeen, some years since tried at the Old Bailey for what there was every reason to think his first offence, acknowledged himself so *delighted with the spirited and heroic character of Macheath, that, on quitting the theatre, he laid out his last guinea in the purchase of a pair of pistols, and stopped a gentleman on the highway !*" *

* Ireland's Hogarth Illustrated, vol. ii. p. 346.

CONQUEST OF MEXICO;

THE scene of the last plate was laid in Newgate; that of the present is a prison in Mexico: a number of children are enacting their respective parts in Dryden's tragedy of the *Indian Emperor; or, the Conquest of Mexico*. The names of the various performers and of the audience being engraved at the foot of the print, we proceed to give an extract from Dryden's play, illustrative of the subject.

The *Indian Emperor* is a continuation or sequel to the *Indian Queen*, which last was jointly written by Dryden and Sir Robert Havard. The Indian Emperor is the production of Dryden's muse, and in rhyme: but,

quantum mutatus ab illo,

it is every way unworthy of that great man's pen; and it has excited *some* astonishment that the ribaldry

which Dryden wrote to gratify the vicious taste of the abandoned Charles II. and his debauched court, should have been perpetuated in a recent edition of the poet's collective works. The following are the extracts above referred to; they are taken from the fourth scene (a prison) of act iv. The dramatis personæ are Cortez, Cydaria, Almeria, Alibech.

CYDARIA. " More cruel than the tyger o'er his spoil,
And falser than the weeping crocodile ;—
Can you add vanity to guilt, and take
A pride to hear the conquests which you make ?
Go—publish your renown ;—let it be said,
You have a woman, and that love betray'd."

CORTEZ. " With what injustice is my faith accused?
Life! Freedom! Empire! I at once refused;
And would again ten thousand times for you."

ALMERIA. " She'll have too great content to find him true;
And therefore, since his love is not for me,
I'll help to make my rival's misery.
Spaniards! I never thought you false before;
Can you *at once* two mistresses adore ?
Keep the poor soul no longer in suspence,
Your change is such, it does not need defence."

Mr Ireland says, a Mr T. Hill was the prompter; but the figure numbered (15) and referred to him, is stationed among the auditors, and Dr Desaguliers (No. 16) is on the stage rehearsing aloud, in order to assist the memories of these pigmy professors of the buskin. The figures should perhaps be transposed, in order to make the print correspond with the explanation engraved beneath.

THE BENCH.

———

HOGARTH having frequently been censured as a caricaturist, notwithstanding caricature formed no part of his profession, published this print in the year 1758, in order to elucidate *his* views, and to give to the world a just definition of the words *character, caricatura*, and *outré*. But as the plate did not sufficiently answer his purpose, (giving an illustration of *character* only,) he, in October, 1764, added the group of heads above, which he never lived to finish, though he worked upon it the day before his death. It must, however, be admitted that he has not yet succeeded in fully developing his sentiments. The following explanation was engraved at the foot of the large prints, and is now retained, in order that the reader may be put in possession of Hogarth's views on the subject.

" CHARACTER, CARICATURE, AND OUTRÉ."

" THERE are hardly any two things more essentially different than *character* and *caricature*, nevertheless they are usually confounded, and mistaken for each other, on which account this explanation is attempted.

" It has ever been allowed that when a character

THE BENCH.

PL. LXVII.

is strongly marked in the living face, it may be considered as an index of the mind, to express which with any degree of justness in painting requires the utmost efforts of a great master. Now that which has of late years got the name of *caricature* is, or ought to be, totally divested of every stroke that hath a tendency to good drawing; it may be said to be a species of lines that are produced rather by the hand of chance than of skill; for the early scrawlings of a child, which do but barely hint an idea of a human face, will always be found to be like some person or other, and will often form such a comical resemblance, as, in all probability, the most eminent caricatures of these times will not be able to equal with design, because their ideas of objects are so much the more perfect than children's, that they will unavoidably introduce some kind of drawing: for all the humorous effects of the fashionable manner of *caricaturing* chiefly depend on the surprise we are under at finding ourselves caught with any sort of similitude in objects absolutely remote in their kind. Let it be observed, the more remote in their nature, the greater is the excellence of these pieces. As a proof of this, I remember a famous *caricature* of a *certain Italian singer*, that struck at first sight, which consisted only of a straight perpendicular line, with a dot over it. As to the French word *outré*, it is different from the foregoing, and signifies nothing more than the exaggerated outline of a figure, all the parts of which may be, in other respects, a perfect and true picture of human nature. A giant or a dwarf may be called a common man *outré;* so any part, as a nose, or leg, made bigger or less than it ought to be, in the part *outré*, which is all that is to be understood by this word, injudiciously used to the prejudice of *character.*" [*]

The lower part of the plate exhibits the court of Common Pleas, and portraits of the four judges who presided on that bench. The principal figure is the late Lord Chief Justice Willes; on his left hand are Mr Justice Bathurst, and the Hon. William Noel; and on his right is Sir Edward Clive. On the caricatura figures in the upper part, (being left unfinished) it would perhaps be presumptuous to offer any strictures.

[*] See EXCESS, Analysis of Beauty, chap. vi.

BATTLE OF THE PICTURES.

" In curious paintings I'm exceeding nice,
And know their several beauties by their price.
Auctions and sales I constantly attend;
But choose my pictures by a skilful friend.
Originals and copies much the same;
The picture's value is the painter's name."

This was an admission ticket, for persons to bid for Hogarth's works at an auction; and was designed to lash the pompous puffs resorted to by many auctioneers in the disposal of pictures by the hammer.

On the right of the plate we observe an auction-room, on the top of which is a weather-cock, which has been thought to allude to Cock the auctioneer, with whom our artist was, at one time, not on very friendly terms. At the door is stationed a porter, with a huge staff in his hand; and, by way of a shew-board, a highly-finished head (after the Flemish school) is exhibited in a clumsy carved frame. Instead of the ordinary insignia of a sale (a catalogue and piece of carpet.) we here have at the end of a long pole an unfurled standard, blazoned with the auctioneer's arms, "*the fate-deciding hammer*."

Beneath, an Apollo (whose godship is discernible only by the rays around his brow) is flaying Marsyas the satyr, who seems to undergo the operation with perfect indifference. Behind this stands a picture of St Andrew on the cross, with a vast number of fac-similies arranged in goodly order; and by the saint's side is a host of Jupiters and Europas, disposed in a similar manner. These are all marshalled in battle array, as the *unquestionable* productions of the great *Italian masters;* although it is more than probable that some at least of these *genuine originals* were painted by their *disciples.*

On the left of the print, we behold a number of pictures in hostile array. We begin with the founder of the order of Franciscans. The corner of the holy saint's picture is driven through Hogarth's Morning; a weeping Madona is forcing her passage through the third scene of the Harlot's Progress; while the Aldobrandini marriage breaks into the splendid saloon of the disgusted couple in the second scene of Marriage-à-la-mode. Thus far the contest is favourable to the old masters.

The aërial conflict, however, terminates differently. The riotous scene in the Rake's Progress (No. 3) very unceremoniously perforates Titian's Feast of Olympus; and Midnight Modern Conversation penetrates a Bacchanalian of Rubens.

Notwithstanding the figures in these various pictures are so very much reduced, they are etched with great spirit, and are strongly characteristic.

ad of
ith the

emila
g Ma
eratio
a pa
umbe
by the
s. Ca
bal r
ons
e the
git

umbe
th the
ner of
partia
issign
gress
o the
e se
e col

entir
very
lym
rates

pic
with

THE PREACHER

THE FIRE-EATER.

(NEVER BEFORE ENGRAVED.)

THE original picture from which our present engraving was made was in the possession of the late Mr Deuchar, seal engraver, (of Edinburgh,) who had an extensive acquaintance with the fine arts, and by whose kindness we were favoured with the loan of the picture for the present work. Mr D. was fully persuaded that it was an undoubted original of Hogarth's, and, as such, the editor, artist, and proprietors were desirous of rendering their collection of his works as complete as possible. They therefore gladly availed themselves of the opportunity thus offered to introduce the present humorous print. Mr Deuchar's cabinet of paintings having been disposed of by auction, we have not succeeded in ascertaining the present possessor of the picture.

The subject is a display of the fire-eating talent of a professor of legerdemain, who is devouring the blazing tow, to the great amazement of the spectators. The scene is probably in the market-place of a country town, (the court or town-hall of which appears on the right,) and the performer displays his art appositely enough, beneath the sign of a Phœnix rising from the ashes.

The group of spectators is well arranged; and the various degrees of delight, surprise, and astonishment, are strongly delineated in the different countenances. The contented grin of the fat butcher is well contrasted by the open-mouthed advocate, or parson, who stands next him; and the attitude of the man who is blowing the bellows is expressive of pleasure, not unmixed with doubt. The musical performers who accompany the *eater of fire* seem to participate in the humorous scene; and the *ardent* food which the latter is in the habit of *consuming*, does not seem to have reduced him in point of size. His appearance bespeaks him to be a lover of good cheer, which is probably well supported by the liberal contributions of his spectators.

As a great number of mountebanks have at different times attracted the attention and wonder of the public (especially at country fairs) by eating fire, walking on fire, and similar tricks, our readers will probably be gratified by the following concise notice, relative to the method adopted by these professors of the *black-art*, in order to impose on the credulous.

The most celebrated performer in this noble science was our countryman Richardson, who lived in the reign of Charles II., and whose feats were the subject of much conversation on the continent. His secret (as related in the *Journal des Sçavans* for 1680) consisted in the application of the pure spirit of sulphur. With this he rubbed his hands and other parts which were to be exposed to the fire; the epidermis being thereby burned and cauterized, the skin consequently became hardened and capable of resisting the flame.

This, however, is no new thing—Ambrose Paré (or Paræus) assures us, that he tried it on himself; and that, after washing the hands in urine and *unguentum aureum*, any one may safely dip them in melted lead! Paré further adds, that by washing his hands in the juice of onions, he could bear a hot shovel on them, while it melted lead.

UNDERTAKERS' ARMS.

" ET PLURIMA MORTIS IMAGO."

***

" THE company of undertakers beareth sable, an urinal proper, between *twelve quack-heads*, and *twelve cane heads*, or *consultant.* On a chief * nebulæ,† ermine, one complete doctor ‡ issuant checkie, sustaining in his right hand a baton of the second. On his dexter and sinister sides, *two demi-doctors*, issuant of the second, and two *cane heads*, issuant of the third; the first having one eye couchant towards the dexter side of the escutcheon, the second *faced* per pale proper, and gules guardant,—with this motto—*et plurima mortis imago.*" §

* " A *chief* betokeneth a senator, or honourable personage, borrowed from the Greek, and is a word signifying a *head ;* and as the head is the *chief* part in a man, so the *chief* in the escutcheon should be a reward of such only whose high merits have procured them *chief place, esteem,* or *love* amongst men." *Guillim.*

† " The bearing of *clouds* in arms (saith Upton) doth import some excellence."

‡ This was originally mis-spelt *Docter,* but subsequently corrected. Hogarth frequently disregarded orthography.

§ i. e. The general image of death.

2

COMPANY OF UNDERTAKERS

PL. LXIII

London Published as the Act directs by Robert Scholey 46 Paternoster Row.

a!
w:

tra
on
fig
m.o
7
trio
ten
Mrs
nam
at H
wan
Sally
Aug:
Ibbet
succe
arms,
any k
ration
in Mi
cures
The
valier
Johns
the en
of his
publisl

The above *heraldic* illustration of the undertakers' arms was engraven at the bottom of the plate, which was originally published in the year 1736.

Most of the figures here introduced were portraits, although, at this distance of time, we have only been able to ascertain the three principal figures, whom Hogarth has placed in the chief, or most honourable part of the escutcheon.

The central masculine figure in the centre of the trio, (who are sagaciously consulting on the contents of an urinal,) is said to have been designed for Mrs Mapp, a celebrated bone-setter. " Her maiden name was Wallen. Her father was also a bone-setter at Hindon, Wilts ; but quarrelling with him, she wandered about the country, calling herself *crazy Sally*. On her success in her profession she married, August 11, 1736, one Hill Mapp, a servant to Mr Ibbetson, mercer on Ludgate-hill. In most cases her success was rather more owing to the strength of her arms, and the boldness of her undertakings, than to any knowledge of anatomy or skill in chirurgical operations. Many of her advertisements may be found in Mist's Journal, and still more accounts of her cures in the periodical publications of her time." *

The figure on the right of Mrs Mapp is the chevalier Taylor, a noted oculist of that day, whom Dr Johnson has pronounced to be the most ignorant of the empiric tribe. That he was one of the vainest of his species is evident from his Memoirs, which he published in 1761, and in which he styles himself

* Nichols's Hogarth, vol. i. p. 92.

" Ophthalmiater Pontifical, Imperial and Royal, to his late Majesty—to the Pontifical court—to the person of her Imperial Majesty—to the Kings of Poland, Denmark, Sweden, &c.—to the several Electors of the Holy Empire—to the Royal Infant Duke of Parma—to the Prince of Saxe Gotha, Serenissime, Brother to her Royal Highness the Princess Dowager of Wales—to the Prince Royal of Poland —to the late Prince of Orange—to the present Princes of Bavaria, Modena, Lorrain, Brunswick, Anspach, Bareith, Liege, Middlebourgh, Hesse-Cassel, Holstein, Georgia, &c.—Fellow of the College of Physicians in Rome, Professor in Optics, Doctor in Medicine, and Doctor in Chirurgery in several Universities abroad," &c. &c. &c.

The third figure (on the left of Mrs Mapp) is the celebrated Dr Joshua Ward, surnamed Spot Ward, from the circumstance of one of his cheeks being marked with claret.

This gentleman was one of the younger sons of an ancient and respectable family settled at Guisborough in Yorkshire, where he was born some time in the 17th century. He seems, from every description of him, to have had small advantages from education, though he indisputably possessed no mean natural parts. The first account we have of him is, that he was associated in partnership with a brother named William, as a dry-salter, in Thames-street. After they had carried on this business some time, a fire broke out in an adjoining house, which communicated itself to their warehouses, and destroyed all their property. On this occasion Mr Ward, with a

gentleman from the country, who was on a visit to
him, escaped over the tops of the houses in their
shirts. In the year 1717, he was returned member
for Marlborough; but, by a vote of the House of
Commons, dated May 13, was declared not duly
elected. It is imagined that he was in some measure
connected with his brother John Ward, (who is stig-
matized by Mr Pope, Dunciad, iii. 34,) in secreting
and protecting illegally the property of some of the
South Sea Directors. Be this as it may, he soon after
quitted England, resided some years abroad, and has
been frequently supposed to have turned Roman
Catholic. While he remained in exile, he acquired
that knowledge of medicine and chemistry which
afterwards was the means of raising him to a state
of affluence. About the year 1733 he began to practise physic, and combated for some time the united
efforts of wit, learning, argument, ridicule, malice,
and jealousy, by all of which he was opposed in every
shape that can be suggested. At length, by some
lucky cures, and particularly one on a relation of Sir
Joseph Jekyll, Master of the Rolls, he got the better
of his opponents, and was suffered to practise undis-
turbed. From this time his reputation was established: he was exempted, by a vote of the House
of Commons, from being visited by the censors of
the College of Physicians, and was even called in to
the assistance of King George the Second, whose
hand he cured, and received, as a reward, a commission for his nephew the late General Gansel. It
was his custom to distribute his medicines and advice, and even pecuniary assistance, to the poor, at

his house, *gratis*, and thus he acquired considerable popularity. Indeed, in these particulars, his conduct was entitled to every degree of praise. With a stern outside and rough deportment, he was not wanting in benevolence. After a continued series of success, he died December 21, 1761, at a very advanced age; and left the secret of his medicines to Mr Page, member for Chichester, who bestowed them on two charitable institutions, which have derived considerable advantages from them. His will is printed in the Gentleman's Magazine for 1762, vol. xxxii. p. 208.*

Of the other figures in the lower part of the escutcheon, one is said to have been intended for Dr Price Dodd, who was physician to St Bartholomew's Hospital, and died August 6, 1754; and another for Dr Bamber, a celebrated midwife, physician, and anatomist: but they cannot be identified among the sapient group, all whose countenances are marked with all the pomp and gravity so frequently found among the professors of medicine.

* Nichols's Hogarth, vol. i. p. 90.

rable
oduct
stem
ntmg
cess,
ages
Page
n two
sides-
red in
xxiii

escut-
Price
Hos-
or Dr
l ana-
g the
arked
ound

THE CHORUS.

London Published as the Act directs by Robt S Scholey 46 Paternoster Row.

THE CHORUS;

OR,

REHEARSAL OF THE ORATORIO OF JUDITH.

⎯⎯⎯⎯⎯

THIS print was published in 1734, as a receipt ticket for Midnight Modern Conversation; the receipt was afterwards cut off the plate.

Hogarth has here exhibited a number of singers rehearsing the chorus of—" *The world shall bow to the Assyrian throne,*" in Mr Huggins's oratorio of Judith, the music of which was composed by Fesch. The singers of the different parts of bass, tenor, and treble, may easily be distinguished : and it is worthy of remark, that the notes before them are in the same key with the performers' voices.

In no group of faces, perhaps, is there a greater contrast, a more uncommon variety, or a more ridiculous appearance to be found, than that with which we are here presented. Not only the faces, (none of which appear to be designed for portraits,) but also the bodies of the performers, are fully occupied in the laborious task of dividing their time,—heads, shoulders, feet,—all move responsive to the composer's notes. So agitated is the leader of the band, who may be observed above, beating time, that he has been obliged to tie his spectacles round his head, lest they should take their departure. It would have been well if he had taken a similar precaution to secure his wig, which has deserted his head and fallen backwards.

" To paint a sound," (Mr Ireland observes,) " is impossible ; but, as far as art can go towards it, Mr Hogarth has gone in this print. The tenor, treble, and bass of these ear-piercing choristers are so decisively discriminated, that we *all but hear them*." *

* Ireland's Hogarth, vol. ii. 296.

Pl. LXXXII.

SIGISMUNDA.

London, Published as the Act directs by Wm. Hogarth

SIGISMUNDA.

THE circumstances connected with the history of this painting having been detailed in our first volume,* it will (we apprehend) be sufficient to refer the reader thither. By a comparison of the print with what is there stated, the observer will thus be enabled duly to appreciate the artist's merit; and to ascertain whether he has succeeded in pourtraying what Dryden has so admirably described :—

> " Mute, solemn sorrow, free from female noise,
> Such as the majesty of grief destroys."
>
> *Sigismunda and Guiscardo.*

Respecting the melancholy fate of these two unfortunate victims of love and tyranny, it is perhaps unnecessary *here* to say any thing. To give detached passages from Dryden's beautiful tale would far exceed *our* limits : the reader who is desirous of perusing it is therefore referred to that great poet's works.

* Vol. i. p. 14—17.

WILLIAM HOGARTH.

In the year 1758, Hogarth published a full-length portrait of himself painting the comic muse, which was inscribed, " W. Hogarth, Serjeant Painter to his Majesty."—" Engraved by W. Hogarth." But this being a mistake of the writing engraver, he afterwards altered it three different times; and in its present (or fifth) state it was published in 1764.

For an account of this distinguished artist, our readers will consult the earlier part of our first volume.

A
stu
exa
thi
smi
her
part
witl
mad
T
subs
figu
estin
artis
havi
to th
tions
publ
than
price
alten
to th
from
leaci
vo

BOYS
PEEPING AT NATURE.

(SEE THE VIGNETTE IN THE ENGRAVED TITLE TO THIS VOLUME.)

A GROUP of young artists is here introduced at their studies. One is intently reading; while a second is examining the proportions of an outline; and the third, whose countenance is marked by a roguish smile, is copying *Nature* herself. The goddess is here delineated as a three-quarter bust, the lower part covered with drapery, and her bosom covered with breasts, referring to the abundant provision made by nature throughout the animated world.

This plate was originally published in 1733, as a subscription ticket to the Harlot's Progress. The figures however were rather too ludicrous in the estimation of some of Hogarth's friends; and the artist threw it aside at their suggestion. In 1751, having etched the burlesque *Paul* as a receipt ticket to the large " *Paul and Felix,*" he found the applications for the gratuitous etching so frequent, that the public were more eager to possess his little print than either of his large ones. He therefore fixed the price of the burlesque Paul at five shillings; and altered the *Boys peeping at Nature* for a receipt ticket to the great picture of Paul. Our engraving is made from the last-mentioned copy, from which the indelicacies are removed.

VOL. II.   Q

THE TIMES.

PLATE I.

THE origin of this political print, and the dispute to which it gave rise between the Painter, Wilkes, and Churchill, have already been stated.* We now proceed to state the various figures introduced, and the probable allusions it contains.

Europe is on fire; France, Germany, Spain, in flames, which are extending to Great Britain. This desolation is continued and assisted by Mr Pitt, under the figure of King Henry VIII. with bellows increasing the mischief which others are striving to abate. He is mounted on the stilts of the populace. A Cheshire cheese † depends from his neck, with 3000*l.* on it. This alludes to what he had said in parliament—that he would sooner live on a Cheshire cheese and a shoulder of mutton, than submit to the enemies of Great Britain. Lord Bute, attended by English soldiers, sailors, and Highlanders, ma-

* Vol. i. p. 22, 23.

† Mr Ireland, with more probability, calls it a mill-stone, and thinks it intimates that so ponderous a load must in time sink his popularity.

nages an engine for extinguishing the flames; but is impeded by the Duke of Newcastle, with a wheelbarrow full of *Monitors* and *North Britons*, for the purpose of feeding the blaze. The respectable body under Mr Pitt are the Aldermen of London, worshipping the idol they had set up; whilst the musical King of Prussia, who alone is sure to gain by the war, is amusing himself with a violin amongst his miserable countrywomen. The picture of the Indian alludes to the advocates for retaining our West Indian conquests, which, it was said, would only increase excess and debauchery. The breaking down of the Newcastle arms, and the drawing up the patriotic ones, refer to the resignation of that noble Duke, and the appointment of his successor. The Dutchman smoking his pipe, and a Fox peeping out behind him, and waiting the issue; the waggon, with the treasures of the Hermione; the unnecessary marching of the militia, signified by the Norfolk jig; the dove with the olive-branch, and the miseries of war, are all obvious, and perhaps need no explication.*

* Nichols's Hogarth, vol. ii. p. 245, where it is taken from the London Magazine for September, 1762. In a newspaper of that day occurs the following humorous description of the characters, whom the anonymous writer asserts to have been really intended.

"The principal figure in the character of Henry VIII. appears to be not Mr Pitt, but another person whose power is signified by his bulk of carcase, treading on Mr Pitt, represented by 3000*l*. The bellows may signify his well-meaning, though ineffectual, endeavours to extinguish the fire by wind, which, though it will put out a small flame, will cherish a large one. The guider of the engine-pipe, I should think, can only mean his majesty, who unweariedly tries, by a more proper method, to stop the flames of war, in which he is

The print (both Mr Wilkes and Mr Ireland have observed) is too much crowded with figures; and in this remark our readers, we think, will readily concur.

assisted by all his good subjects, both by sea and land, notwithstanding any interruption from *Auditors* or *Britons, Monitors* or *North Britons.* The respectable body at the bottom can never mean the magistrates of London ; Mr Hogarth has more sense than to abuse so respectable a body ; much less can it mean the judges. I think it may as likely be the Court of Session in Scotland, either in the attitude of adoration, or with outspread arms intending to catch their patron, should his stilts give way. The Frenchman may very well sit at his ease among his miserable countrywomen, as he is not unacquainted that France has always gained by negotiating what she lost in fighting. The fine gentleman at the window with his garretteers, and the barrow of periodical papers, refer to the present contending parties of every denomination. The breaking of the Newcastle arms alludes to the resignation of a great personage ; and the replacing of them, by the sign of the four clenched fists, may be thought emblematical of the great œconomy of his successor. The Norfolk jig signifies, in a lively manner, the alacrity of all his majesty's forces during the war ; and *G. T.* [*George Townshend*] *fecit,* is an opportune compliment paid to Lord Townshend, who, in conjunction with Mr Windham, published " A Plan of Discipline for the Use of the Norfolk Militia ;" and had been the greatest advocate for the establishment of our present militia. The Picture of the Indian alive from America, is a satire on our late uncivilized behaviour to the three chiefs of the *Cherokee* nation, who were lately in this kingdom ; and the bags of money set this in a still clearer point of view, signifying the sums gained by shewing them at our public gardens. The sly Dutchman, with his pipe, seems pleased with the combustion, from which he thinks he shall be a gainer. And the Duke of Nivernois, under the figure of a dove, is coming from France to give a cessation of hostilities to Europe." Ibid, and J. Ireland's Hogarth, vol. i. p. 236.

THE TIMES. N.º2.

London Published as the Act directs by Robert Sayer, 53 Fleet Street Pall Mall.

PLATE II.

THE TIMES.

THE publication of the preceding print having involved Hogarth in a contest with two adepts in the use of the PEN, the artist had no means of retaliation but the copper-plate and implements of his profession. To these he resorted, and produced the two plates which will next be described. The present, though engraved during Hogarth's life-time, was never published; nor would Mrs Hogarth suffer it to be made public, for reasons which it would now be needless to state, and perhaps fruitless to ascertain. At the earnest persuasion of Lord Exeter, she permitted one impression only to be taken off.

After the decease of Mrs Hogarth, Messrs Boydell purchased the plate, which was published in 1790. Our description of it is abridged from Mr Ireland's very able illustrations of this political satire.

On a pedestal in the centre of the print is a statue of the present king, in his coronation robes. On the front of the pedestal is the head of a lion, in bas relief, with a leaden pipe in his mouth. A figure turning a fire-plug represents Lord Bute. A baronial escutcheon, keys, stars, coronets, croziers, mitres, maces, lie close to the pedestal, around which are placed several garden-pots with shrubs. Two rose-trees, most plentifully sprinkled by streams from the fountain of favour, have been originally inscribed *James III.*; but, *James* being now blotted out, *George* is put above it, and, by a little hyphen beneath the lowest figure, marked as belonging to the lowest line. Three orange-trees have the initials *G. R.*; and beneath the letters is inscribed *Republican*. These also receive drops of favour: but a large laurel, planted in a capacious vase, and inscribed *Colloden*, is watered by the dew of heaven—by a copious shower poured from the urn of Aquarius. Besides these six flourishing plants, there are a number of yew and box trees, clipped into *true taste* by a Dutch gardener. Some of them retain their old situations; but an active labourer is busily clearing the grounds of all these *ancient formalities*. Many of them he has already wheeled out of their places, and thrown into the ditch that surrounds the platform, into which he is now tumbling two venerable box-trees of a most *orderly* and *regular cut*; each of them having the letters *G. R.*; expressing, allegorically, the great number of old placemen who resigned on the accession of his present majesty. The only person on the platform, except Lord Bute, is his great antagonist Mr Henry Fox, afterwards Lord Holland, who is employed in removing the garden-pots. A group on the right hand corner is made up principally of members of the upper house. In the chair, under the king's arms, is Sir John Cust, the Speaker. Under him, wiping his forehead, is William Duke of Cumberland: below whom is Lord Mansfield; and still lower, Lord Temple, offering his snuff-box to the

Duke of Newcastle. The Earl of Winchelsea, distinguished by a ribbon, shews only his back. The figure on his left is supposed to be the Duke of Bedford. The interrogating figure, with a hat on, is Mr Rigby; a gentleman remarkably round, Lord Melcombe; the noble Lord beneath him, the Duke of Devonshire; and the grave Senator in spectacles, the Earl of Bath. The persons *asleep* are not known. On the other side of the rail, among the figures firing at Peace, Mr Pitt, with a long gun, is easily distinguishable. Below him *a Trimmer*, in the act of desertion. The next figure resembles Henry Bilson Legge; and the band with an ear-trumpet is perhaps the Earl of Chesterfield. Two figures distinguished by a muff and a pair of spectacles are not known. The lowest figure resembles the first Lord Holland; but *he* is exhibited on the platform. On the dog immediately behind Lord Bute is written *mercy*, allusive, probably, to 1745. In the opposite group, two personages are placed in the pillory. Over the figure of *Fanny the Phantom*, dressed in a white sheet, is written *Conspiracy.* In one hand she holds a small hammer, and in the other a lighted paper, with which she sets fire to a *North Briton* that is fastened to the breast of *John Wilkes*, over whose head is written *defamation :* and who is depicted with a most rueful countenance and empty pockets. Among the crowd below are a Highlander; a Lilliputian chimney-sweeper; a fellow blowing a cow's horn; a woman retailing gin from a keg marked *J. W.*; and a school-boy amusing himself *à la Teniers* with Mr Wilkes's shoes; whilst an Abigail is trundling a mop over his head. The group

below consists of sailors and soldiers. Archbishop
Secker is represented, confirming two adults. At
the rooms where the Society of Arts, &c. then met,
a number of persons, by the help of a crane, are
dragging up a large *silver pallette*, on which is written *premium*. The man instructing the workman is
Dr Templeman, then Secretary; and on the first floor
is Lord Romney, their president. Behind this is the
new church in the Strand : on the opposite side, a
triumphal column; a structure with the word *Hospital* in the front; and a scaffolding with workmen,
completing a new building, in which Hogarth anti-
cipated the present *Somerset-house.*

* Mr J. Ireland's Hogarth, vol. ii. p. 265, *et seq.*

Pl. LXXVII.

London Published as the Act directs by Robert Sayer, at Bartram & Son.

THE BRUISER.

CHARLES CHURCHILL,

(ONCE THE REVEREND,)

IN THE CHARACTER OF A RUSSIAN HERCULES.

———————

IRRITATED by the publication of Mr Wilkes's portrait, (see p. 93,) Churchill published a malignant epistle to the painter, which called forth all his pictorial powers of retaliation. Hogarth took a plate on which he had some time before engraved his portrait, together with that of his favourite dog, Trump, and expunging his own head, he substituted that of Churchill, dressed with a tattered band and torn ruffles, in the character of a Russian bear.—Beneath the print he inserted the following words :—

" A Russian Hercules (yet no small likeness of the man) regaling himself after having killed the monster *Caracatura*, that so sorely galled his *virtuous* friend, the *heaven-bórn* Wilkes."

In order to enter into the spirit of this print, it should be observed, that the person of Churchill was stout, lusty, and rough; his shoulders were broad, and his manners as rough and uncouth as his person. The poet's predilection for liquor is admirably intimated by his hugging the tankard of porter, and by the drops which fall from his mouth. The ragged band alludes to his clerical profession (which he afterwards renounced); and the mutilated ruffles to the frays in which he was not unfrequently involved. With his left paw he grasps a knotted club, with the letters N. B. on it towards the top, referring to the celebrated political paper, the *North Briton*, in which Churchill assisted Wilkes. On this club (referring to the political falsehoods the North Briton contained), Hogarth wrote on the large prints, "*Infamous Fallacy,*" and has numbered its knots as so many notorious lies.

The picture is raised from the floor (on which lie the palette and burin, emblematic of the artist's profession), by three books, on the uppermost of which is written, *A List of Subscribers to the North Briton*; and on another, *A new Way to pay old Debts, by Massinger.* To intimate the poverty of the writer, the *pedestal* is crowned by a begging-box. On the opposite side, Trump tramples on the poet's epistle to the painter, which he treats most contemptuously, in a manner that is not natural to the canine species.

The small drawing or picture on the palette was not in this plate when first published; being subsequently added, in order to refute the calumnious assertion that the painter was in his dotage.

Mr Pitt is represented reclining at his ease with a mill-stone hanging over his head, on which is written 3000*l.*; * and firing a mortar at a dove bearing an olive-branch, (the symbol of peace,) which is perched over the standard of England.   He is attended by the two giants from Guildhall, with pipes in their mouths, referring to the support which the city of London uniformly gave to this great statesman,—— and more particularly the late opulent Alderman Beckford, who enjoyed the rare felicity of being three times Lord Mayor.   One of these giants is placing a crown on Mr Pitt's head, while the other holds in his hand a shield containing the arms of Austria, which the hero spurns with contempt from his feet.

On the opposite side of the print Hogarth makes his entry as a shewman, leading Wilkes in the character of a *monkey*, riding on a stick, with a cap of liberty on the top of it, and the North Briton in his hand ; while Churchill advances as a muzzled bear, decorated with ruffles and a band, and a laced hat upon his head.   The artist is flogging them, and makes them keep time to the sweet scrapings of a fiddler devoid of features, who is said to have been Earl Temple.   The satire contained in this tablet abundantly answered the artist's purpose, and was greatly admired by the public.

We have stated above that our ingenious artist painted the picture here described by way of retaliation on Churchill ; how justly the poet deserved such

---

* This refers to his saying that Hanover was a mill-stone round the neck of England, on account of the expences incurred by keeping that electorate, and his afterwards *augmenting* the public expences by accepting a pension of 3000*l.* per annum.

a retaliating scourge the reader will be at no loss to
conceive after perusing the following lines, extract-
ed from the poet's epistle to the painter :

" With all the symptoms of assur'd decay,
With age and sickness pinch'd and worn away,
Pale quiv'ring lips, lank cheeks, and falt'ring tongue,
The spirits out of tune, the nerves unstrung,
The body shrivell'd up, the dim eyes sunk
Within their sockets deep, the weak hams shrunk,
The body's weight unable to sustain,
The streams of life scarce trembling through the vein,
More than half kill'd by honest truths which fell
Through thy own fault from men who wish'd thee well;
Canst thou, even thus, thy thoughts to vengeance give,
And, dead to all things else, to malice live?—
Hence, dotard, to thy closet—shut thee in,
By deep repentance wash away thy sin;
From haunts of men to shame and sorrow fly,
And on the verge of death learn how to die." *

* Works, vol. i. p. 146, 4to. edition, (1765.)

055 W
tract

JOHN WILKS ESQ.

London Published as the Act directs by Robert Scholey 46 Paternoster Row.

JOHN WILKES, ESQ.

———

Tʜɪꜱ portrait has been called a caricature and a satire upon the celebrated demagogue whose name it
bears, though we are unable to ascertain the reason
why it has been so considered. The artist had abundant cause of provocation to have caricatured him,
if he had been so disposed; but the fact is, that the
print is an excellent likeness of Mr Wilkes, which
was taken by Hogarth in Westminster Hall, on that
memorable day when the former, after being a second
time brought thither from the Tower, was honour-
ably acquitted.

At the time the artist drew this portrait, Wilkes
was in the zenith of his popularity: the accompaniments therefore are well suited to the occasion:
they consist of the cap of liberty, which he is twirl-
ing on a stick, and Nos. 17 and 45 of the North Briton, which lie on the table.

So great was the demand for this portrait on its
first publication in 1763, that nearly 4,000 copies
were disposed of in a short time.

THE BATHOS;

FINIS, OR THE END OF TIME.

———

THE circumstances which led to the production of this admirable picture having already been stated,[*] we now proceed to point out its design.

This is two-fold:—*first*, to collect together such objects as denoted the *end* of time;—and, *secondly*, to ridicule the gross absurdities which are to be seen in the serious works of some of the ancient masters, who have blended the grave with the sublime, and the trifling with subjects of importance. Alluding to Swift's humorous *art of sinking in poetry*, Hogarth called it THE BATHOS, *or manner of sinking in sublime paintings*, and inscribed the plate to the dealers in dark pictures.

As there is no great connexion among the variety of objects we observe in this print, excepting a conformity with the end, we shall mention the various articles as they present themselves to our view. On

[*] See vol. i. p. 20.

THE RADISH

the right is a ruinous tower, having a decayed time-piece or dial-plate in front; contiguous to that is a tomb-stone decorated with a death's head, and, leaning on the remains of a column, we perceive TIME in the utmost agony breathing out his *last ;* his usual accompaniments, the scythe, tube, and hour-glass are broken, his sinews are unstrung, and his course is run. In one hand he holds a parchment scroll, containing his will, in which he has bequeathed every atom of *this* world to Chaos, whom he has appointed sole executor. This *testament* is duly executed by the three sister fates, *Clotho, Lachesis,* and *Atropos.*

Beneath the will of Time lies a shoemaker's *last,* around which is entwined the cobler's *end.* On the right of these, are an empty ragged purse, a commission of bankruptcy, with the seal annexed, supposed to be issued against poor dame *Nature,* and a play-book open at the last page.

In the centre appear a broken bow, a broken crown, and a worn-out scrubbing-brush. On the other side of the plate is opposed a withered tree, beneath which stands an unthatched cottage, together with a falling sign of the *world's end,* described by a terrestrial globe bursting out into flames. At the foot of this print, is our artist's own print of the Times, set on fire by an inch of candle. Near this, a cracked *bell* is contrasted by a broken bottle, a worn-out broom, the stock of a musket, a rope's end, a whip without its lash, a mutilated capital of the Ionic order, and a painter's broken palette. At some distance, a man is gibbeted in chains, and a ship is seen foundering at sea. To complete the whole, in the firma-

ment above, the moon is darkened by the death of
Phœbus, (the sun,) who (with his lifeless coursers)
lies extended on a cloud, while his chariot wheels
are broken, and consequently the source of light is
extinguished.

> " The cloud-capt towers, the gorgeous palaces,
> The solemn temples, the *great globe* itself,
> Yea, all which it inherit, shall dissolve,
> And—like the baseless fabric of a vision—
> Leave not a rack behind."————
>
> Tempest, Act iv. Scene i.

FINIS!

eadh of

oursen

wheea

ligate

Scene.

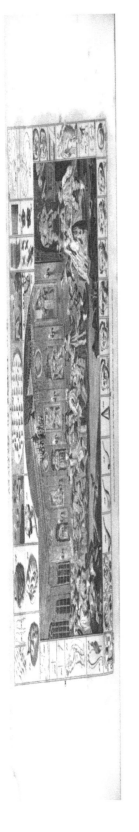

THE

Analysis of Beauty,

WRITTEN

WITH A VIEW TO FIX THE FLUCTUATING
IDEAS OF TASTE.

BY WILLIAM HOGARTH.

VARIETY.

So vary'd he, and of his tortuous train
Curl'd many a wanton wreath, in sight of Eve,
To lure her eye.———   MILTON.

CONTENTS.

PREFACE.

If a preface was ever necessary, it may very likely be thought so to the following work; the title of which (in the proposals published some time since) hath much amused and raised the expectation of the curious, though not without a mixture of doubt, that its purport could ever be satisfactorily answered. For though beauty is seen and confessed by all, yet, from the many fruitless attempts to account for the cause of its being so, enquiries on this head have almost been given up; and the subject generally thought to be a matter of too high and too delicate a nature to admit of any true or intelligible discussion. Something therefore introductory ought to be said at the presenting a work with a face so entirely new, especially as it will naturally encounter with, and perhaps may overthrow, several long-received and thorough-established opinions: and since controversies may arise how far, and after what manner this subject hath hitherto been considered and treated, it will also be proper to lay before the reader what may be

a

gathered concerning it, from the works of the ancient and modern writers and painters.

It is no wonder this subject should have so long been thought inexplicable, since the nature of many parts of it cannot possibly come within the reach of mere men of letters; otherwise those ingenious gentlemen who have lately published treatises upon it (and who have written much more learnedly than can be expected from one who never took up the pen before,) would not so soon háve been bewildered in their accounts of it, and obliged so suddenly to turn into the broad and more beaten path of moral beauty, in order to extricate themselves out of the difficulties they seem to have met with in this; and withal forced for the same reasons to amuse their readers with amazing (but often misapplied) encomiums on deceased painters and their performances; wherein they are continually discoursing of effects instead of developing causes; and after many prettinesses, in very pleasing language, do fairly set you down just where they first took you up; honestly confessing that, as to GRACE, the main point in question, they do not even pretend to know any thing of the matter. And indeed how should they? when it actually requires a practical knowledge of the whole art of painting (sculpture alone not being sufficient), and that too to some degree of eminence, in order to

P. iv

enable any one to pursue the chain of this enquiry through all its parts; which I hope will
be made to appear in the following work.

It will then naturally be asked, why the best.
painters within these two centuries, who by their
works appear to have excelled in grace and
beauty, should have been so silent in an affair
of such seeming importance to the imitative arts
and their own honour? to which I answer, that
it is probable they arrived at that excellence in P. v
their works by the mere dint of imitating, with
great exactness, the beauties of nature, and by
often copying and retaining strong ideas of
graceful antique statues; which might sufficiently serve their purposes as painters, without
their troubling themselves with a farther enquiry
into the particular causes of the effects before
them. It is not indeed a little strange, that the
great Leonardo da Vinci (amongst the many
philosophical precepts which he hath at random
laid down in his treatise on painting) should not
have given the least hint of any thing tending to
a system of this kind, especially as he was
contemporary with Michael Angelo, who is said
to have discovered a certain principle in the
trunk only of an antique statue ,(well known
from this circumstance by the name of Michael
Angelo's Torso, or Back, fig. *), which principle

* Fig. 54. p. 1.

gave his works a grandeur of gusto equal to the best antiques. Relative to which tradition, Lamozzo, who wrote about painting at the same time, hath this remarkable passage, vol. i. book 1.

" And because in this place there falleth out a certaine precept of *Michael Angelo* much for our purpose, I wil not conceale it, leaving the farther interpretation and vnderstanding thereof to the iudicious reader. It is reported, then, that *Michael Angelo* vpon a time gaue this observation to the painter *Marcus de Sciena* his scholler, *that he should alwaies make a figure pyramidall, serpentlike, and multiplied by one, two, and three.* In which precept (in mine opinion) the whole mysterie of the arte consisteth ; for the greatest grace and life that a picture can haue is, that it expresse *motion ;* which the painters call the *spirite* of a picture. Nowe there is no forme so fitte to expresse this *motion,* as that of the flame of fire, which, according to *Aristotle* and the other philosophers, is an elemente most actiue of all others ; because the forme of the flame thereof is most apt for motion ; for it hath a *conus,* or sharpe pointe, wherewith it seemeth to divide the aire, that so it may ascende to his proper sphere. So that a picture having this forme will bee most beautifull *."

* See Haydock's translation, printed at Oxford, 1598.

Many writers since Lamozzo have, in the same words, recommended the observing this rule also, without comprehending the meaning of it; for unless it were known systematically, the whole business of grace could not be understood.

Du Fresnoy, in his Art of Painting, says, " large flowing, gliding outlines, which are in waves, give not only a grace to the part, but to the whole body, as we see in the Antinous, and in many other of the antique figures: a fine figure and its parts ought always to have a serpent-like and flaming form ; naturally those sort P. vii of lines have I know not what of life and seeming motion in them, which very much resembles the activity of the flame and of the serpent." Now, if he had understood what he had said, he could not, speaking of grace, have expressed himself in the following contradictory manner: —" But, to say the truth, this is a difficult undertaking, and a rare present, which the artist rather receives from the hand of heaven than from his own industry and studies *." But De

* See Dryden's translation of his Latin poem on Painting, verse 28, and the remarks on these very lines, page 155, which run thus:—" It is difficult to say what this grace of painting is ; it is to be conceived and understood much more easy than to be expressed by words ; it proceeds from the il-

Piles, in his Lives of the Painters, is still more contradictory, where he says, " that a painter can only have it (meaning grace) from nature, and doth not know that he hath it, nor in what degree, nor how he communicates it to his works : and that grace and beauty are two different things ; beauty pleases by the rules, and grace without them."

All the English writers on this subject have echoed these passages ; hence *Je ne sçai quoi* is become a fashionable phrase for grace.

By this it is plain, that this precept, which Michael Angelo delivered so long ago in an oracle-like manner, hath remained mysterious down to this time, for aught that has appeared to the contrary. The wonder that it should do so will in some measure lessen when we come to consider that it must all along have appeared as P.viii full of contradiction as the most obscure quibble ever delivered at Delphos, because *winding lines are as often the cause of deformity as of grace*, the solution of which in this place would be an anticipation of what the reader will find at large in the body of the work.

There are also strong prejudices in favour of straight lines, as constituting true beauty in the

luminations of an excellent mind, (but not to be acquired), by which we give a certain turn to things, which makes them pleasing."

human form, where they never should appear.
A middling connoisseur thinks no profile has
beauty without a very straight nose; and if the
forehead be continued straight with it, he thinks
it is still more sublime. I have seen miserable
scratches with the pen sell at a considerable
rate for only having in them a side-face or two,
like that between fig. 22 and fig. 105, plate 1,
which was made, and any one might do the
same, with the eyes shut. The common notion
that a person should be straight as an arrow,
and perfectly erect, is of this kind. If a dancing-master were to see his scholar in the easy
and gracefully-turned attitude of the Antinous
(fig. 6, plate 1,) he would cry shame on him,
and tell him he looked as crooked as a ram's
horn, and bid him hold up his head as he himself did. See fig. 7, plate 1.

The painters in like manner, by their works,
seem to be no less divided upon the subject than
the authors. The French, except such as have
imitated the antique or the Italian school, seem
to have studiously avoided the serpentine line
in all their pictures, especially Anthony Coypel,
history painter, and Rigaud, principal portrait-
painter, to Lewis the 14th.

Rubens, whose manner of designing was P. ix
quite original, made use of a large flowing line
as a principle, which runs through all his works,

and gives a noble spirit to them ; but he did not seem to be acquainted with what we call the *precise line ;* which hereafter we shall be very particular upon, and which gives the delicacy we see in the best Italian masters ; but he rather charged his contours in general with too bold and S-like swellings.

Raphael, from a straight and stiff manner, on a sudden changed his taste of lines at sight of Michael Angelo's works, and the antique statues ; and so fond was he of the serpentine line, that he carried it into a ridiculous excess, particularly in his draperies ; though his great observance of nature suffered him not long to continue in this mistake.

Peter de Cortone formed a fine manner in his draperies of this line.

We see this principle no where better understood than in some pictures of Corregio, particularly his Juno and Ixion ; yet the proportions of his figures are sometimes such as might be corrected by a common sign-painter.

Whilst Albert Durer, who drew mathematically, never so much as deviated into grace, which he must sometimes have done in copying the life, if he had not been fettered with his own impracticable rules of proportion.

P. x　　But that which may have puzzled this matter most may be, that Vandyke, one of the best portrait painters in most respects ever known, plainly appears not to have had a thought of this kind. For there seems not to be the least grace in his pictures more than what the life chanced to bring before him. There is a print of the Duchess of Wharton, (fig. 52, plate 2,) engraved by Van Gunst, from a true picture by him, which is thoroughly divested of every elegance. Now, had he known this line as a principle, he could no more have drawn all the parts of this picture so contrary to it, than Mr Addison could have wrote a whole Spectator in false grammar; unless it were done on purpose. However, on account of his other great excellencies, painters chuse to style this want of grace in his attitudes, &c. *simplicity,* and indeed they do often very justly merit that epithet.

Nor have the painters of the present times been less uncertain and contradictory to each other than the masters already mentioned, whatever they may pretend to the contrary: of this I had a mind to be certain, and therefore, in the year 1745, published a frontispiece to my engraved works, in which I drew a serpentine line lying on a painter's pallet, with these words under it, THE LINE OF BEAUTY. The bait soon took; and no Egyptian hieroglyphic ever amused more than it did for a time; painters and sculptors came to me to know the meaning of it, P. xi being as much puzzled with it as other people, till it came to have some explanation; then indeed, but not till then, some found it out to be an old acquaintance of theirs, though the account they could give of its properties was very near as satisfactory as that which a day-labourer, who constantly uses the leaver, could give of that machine as a mechanical power.

Others, as common face-painters and copiers of pictures, denied that there could be such a rule either in art or nature, and asserted it was all stuff and madness; but no wonder that these gentlemen should not be ready in comprehending a thing they have little or no business with. For though the *picture-copier* may sometimes to a common eye seem to vie with the original he copies, the artist himself requires no more ability, genius, or knowledge of nature than a journeyman weaver at the goblins, who, in working after a piece of painting bit by bit, scarcely knows what he is about, whether he is weaving a man or a horse, yet at last almost insensibly turns out of his loom a fine piece of tapestry, representing, it may be, one of Alexander's battles painted by Le Brun.

As the above-mentioned print thus involved me in frequent disputes by explaining the qualities of the line, I was extremely glad to find it (which I had conceived as only part of a system

8

in my mind) so well supported by the above precept of Michael Angelo : which was first pointed out to me by Dr Kennedy, a learned antiquarian and connoisseur, of whom I afterwards purchased the translation, from which I have taken several passages to my purpose.

Let us now endeavour to discover what light antiquity throws upon the subject in question.

Egypt first, and afterward Greece, have manifested by their works their great skill in arts and sciences, and, among the rest, painting and sculpture, all which are thought to have issued from their great schools of philosophy. Pythagoras, Socrates, and Aristotle seem to have pointed out the right road in nature for the study of the painters and sculptors of those times, (which they in all probability afterwards followed through those nicer paths that their particular professions required them to pursue,) as may be reasonably collected from the answers given by Socrates to Aristippus his disciple, and Parrhasius the painter, concerning FITNESS, the first fundamental law in nature with regard to beauty.

I am in some measure saved the trouble of collecting an historical account of these arts among the ancients, by accidentally meeting with a preface to a tract called the *Beau Ideal* : this treatise*

---

* Published in 1732, and sold by A. Millar.

was written by Lambert Hermanson Ten Kate, in French, and translated into English by James Christopher le Blon ; who in that preface says, speaking of the author, " His superior know- P. xiii ledge that I am now publishing is the product of the Analogy of the ancient Greeks ; or the true key for finding all harmonious proportions in painting, sculpture, architecture, music, &c. brought home to Greece by Pythagoras. For after this great philosopher had travelled into Phœnicia, Egypt, and Chaldea, where he con- versed with the learned, he returned into Greece about *Anno Mundi* 3484, before the Christian æra 520, and brought with him many excellent discoveries and improvements for the good of his countrymen, among which the Analogy was one of the most considerable and useful.

" After him the Grecians, by the help of this Analogy, began (and not before) to excel other nations in sciences and arts ; for whereas before this time they represented their *Divinities* in plain human figures, the Grecians now began to enter into the Beau Ideal ; and Pamphilus, (who flourished *A. M.* 3641, before the Christian æra 363, who taught, that no man could excel in painting without mathematics,) the scholar of Pausius and master of Apelles, was the first who artfully applied the said Analogy to the art of painting ; as much about the same time the sculpturers, the architects, &c. began to apply it to their several arts, without which science the Grecians had remained as ignorant as their forefathers.

" They carried on their improvements in P.xiv drawing, painting, architecture, sculpture, &c. till they became the wonders of the world ; especially after the Asiatics and Egyptians (who had formerly been the teachers of the Grecians) had, in process of time, and by the havock of war, lost all the excellency in sciences and arts ; for which all other nations were afterwards obliged to the Grecians, without being able so much as to imitate them.

" For when the Romans had conquered Greece and Asia, and had brought to Rome the best paintings and the finest artists, we do not find they discovered the great key of knowledge, the Analogy I am now speaking of ; but their best performances were conducted by Grecian artists, who, it seems, cared not to communicate their secret of the Analogy ; because either they intended to be necessary at Rome, by keeping the secret among themselves, or else the Romans, who principally affected universal dominion, were not curious enough to search after the secret, not knowing the importance of it, nor understanding that, without it, they could never attain to the excellency of the Grecians : though nevertheless it must be owned that the

Romans used well the proportions, which the Grecians long before had reduced to certain fixed rules according to their ancient Analogy; and the Romans could arrive at the happy use P. xv of the proportions, without comprehending the Analogy itself."

This account agrees with what is constantly observed in Italy, where the Greek and Roman work, both in medals and statues, are as distinguishable as the characters of the two languages.

As the preface had thus been of service to me, I was in hopes, from the title of the book, (and the assurance of the translator, that the author had by his great learning discovered the secret of the ancients,) to have met with something there that might have assisted, or confirmed the scheme I had in hand; but was much disappointed in finding nothing of that sort, and no explanation, or even after-mention, of what at first agreeably alarmed me, the word *Analogy*. I have given the reader a specimen in his own words how far the author has discovered this grand secret of the ancients, or *great key of knowledge*, as the translator calls it.

" The sublime part that I so much esteem, and of which I have begun to speak, is a real *Je ne sçai quoi*, or an unaccountable something to most people, and it is the most important part to all the connoisseurs, I shall call it an harmonious propriety, which is a touching or moving unity, or a pathetic agreement or concord, not only of each member to its body, but also of each part to the member of which it is a part : *It is also an infinite variety of parts*, however conformable with respect to each different P. xvi subject, so that all the attitude, and all the adjustment of the draperies of each figure, ought to answer or correspond to the subject chosen. Briefly, it is a true decorum, a bienseance or a congruent disposition of ideas, as well for the face and stature, as for the attitudes. A bright genius, in my opinion, who aspires to excel in the ideal, should propose this to himself, as what has been the principal study of the most famous artists. 'Tis in this part that the great masters cannot be imitated or copied but by themselves, or by those that are advanced in the knowledge of the ideal, and who are as knowing as those masters in the rules or laws of the pittoresque and poetical nature, although inferior to the masters in the high spirit of invention."

The words in this quotation, " *It is also an infinite variety of parts*," seem at first to have some meaning in them, but it is entirely destroyed by the rest of the paragraph, and all the other pages are filled, according to custom, with descriptions of pictures.

Now, as every one has a right to conjecture

what this discovery of the ancients might be, it shall be my business to shew it was a key to the thorough knowledge of variety both in form and movement. Shakespear, who had the deepest penetration into nature, has summed up all the xvii charms of beauty in two words, INFINITE VARIETY; where, speaking of Cleopatra's power over Anthony, he says,

———Nor custom stale
Her infinite variety :———   Act 2. Scene 3.

It has been ever observed, that the ancients made their doctrines mysterious to the vulgar, and kept them secret from those who were not of their particular sects and societies, by means of symbols and hieroglyphics. Lamozzo says, chap. 29, book 1. " The Grecians, in imitation of antiquity, searched out the truly renowned proportion, wherein the exact perfection of most exquisite beauty and sweetness appeareth ; dedicating the same, in a triangular glass, unto Venus, the goddess of divine beauty, from whence all the beauty of inferior things is derived."

If we suppose this passage to be authentic, may we not also imagine it probable, that the symbol in the triangular glass might be similar to the line Michael Angelo recommended ; especially if it can be proved that the triangular form of the glass, and the serpentine line it-self, are the two most expressive figures that can be thought of to signify not only beauty and grace, but the whole *order of form*.

There is a circumstance in the account Pliny gives of Apelles's visit to Protogenes, which strengthens this supposition. I hope I may have leave to repeat the story. Apelles having heard of the fame of Protogenes, went to Rhodes to pay him a visit, but not finding P him at home, asked for a board, on which he drew a *line*, telling the servant maid, that line would signify to her master who had been to see him; we are not clearly told what sort of a line it was that could so particularly signify one of the first of his profession: if it was only a stroke (though as fine as a hair, as Pliny seems to think,) it could not possibly by any means denote the abilities of a great painter. But if we suppose it to be a line of some extraordinary quality, such as the serpentine line will appear to be, Apelles could not have left a more satisfactory signature of the compliment he had paid him. Protogenes, when he came home, took the hint, and drew a finer, *or rather more expressive line*, within it, to shew Apelles, if he came again, that he understood his meaning. He, soon returning, was well pleased with the answer Protoge-

nes had left for him, by which he was convinced that fame had done him justice, and so,
correcting the line again, perhaps by making
it more precisely elegant, he took his leave.
The story thus may be reconciled to common
sense, which, as it has been generally received,
could never be understood but as a ridiculous
tale.

Let us add to this, that there is scarce an
Egyptian, Greek, or Roman deity, but hath a
twisted serpent, twisted cornucopia, or some
symbol winding in this manner, to accompany
it. The two small heads (over the busto of the
P.xix Hercules, fig. 4, in plate 1.) of the goddess Isis,
one crowned with a globe between two horns,
the other with a lily *, are of this kind. Har-
pocrates, the god of silence, is still more remarkably so, having a large twisted horn growing out
of the side of his head, one cornucopia in his
hand, and another at his feet, with his finger
placed on his lips, indicating secrecy. (See
Montfaucon's Antiquities). And it is as remarkable, that the deities of barbarous and

* The leaves of this flower as they grow, twist themselves
various ways in a pleasing manner, as may be better seen by
figure 43, in plate 1 ; but there is a curious little flower, called the Autumn Syclamen, fig. 47, the leaves of which elegantly twist one way only.

Gothic nations never had, nor have to this day, any of these elegant forms belonging to them. How absolutely void of these turns are the pagods of China, and what a mean taste runs through most of their attempts in painting and sculpture, notwithstanding they finish with such excessive neatness ! the whole nation in these matters seem to have but one eye : this mischief naturally follows from the prejudices they imbibe by copying one another's works, which the ancients seem seldom to have done.

Upon the whole, it is evident that the ancients studied these arts very differently from the moderns. Lamozzo seems to be partly aware of this, by what he says in the division of his work, page 9 : " There is a two-folde proceeding in all artes and sciences ; the one is called the order of nature, and the other of teaching. Nature proceedeth ordinarily, be- P. xxi ginning with the unperfect, as the particulars, and ending with the perfect, as the universals. Now, if, in searching out the nature of things, our understanding shall proceede after that order, by which they are brought forth by nature, doubtlesse it will be the most absolute and ready method that can bee imagined. For we beginne to know things by their first and immediate principles, &c. ; and this is not only

s

mine opinion but Aristotle's also ;" yet, mistaking Aristotle's meaning, and absolutely deviating from his advice, he afterwards says, " all which if we could comprehend within our understanding, we should be most wise ; but it is *impossible*," and after having given some dark reasons why he thinks so, he tells you " he resolves to follow the order of teaching," which all the writers on painting have in like manner since done.

Had I observed the foregoing passage before I undertook this essay, it probably would have put me to a stand, and deterred me from venturing upon what Lamozzo calls an impossible task : but observing in the forementioned controversies that the torrent generally ran against me, and that several of my opponents had turned my arguments into ridicule, yet were daily availing themselves of their use, and venting them even to my face as their own, I began to wish the publication of something on this P. xxi subject ; and accordingly applied myself to several of my friends, whom I thought capable of taking up the pen for me, offering to furnish them with materials by word of mouth ; but finding this method not practicable, from the difficulty of one man's expressing the ideas of another, especially on a subject which he was either unacquainted with, or was new in its kind, I was therefore reduced to an attempt of finding such words as would best answer my own ideas, being now too far engaged to drop the design. Hereupon, having digested the matter as well as I could, and thrown it into the form of a book, I submitted it to the judgment of such friends whose sincerity and abilities I could best rely on, determining on their approbation or dislike to publish or destroy it; but their favourable opinion of the manuscript being publicly known, it gave such a credit to the undertaking as soon changed the countenances of those who had a better opinion of my pencil than my pen, and turned their sneers into expectation; especially when the same friends had kindly made me an offer of conducting the work through the press. And here I must acknowledge myself particularly indebted to one gentleman for his corrections and amendment of at least a third part of the wording. Through his absence and avocations, several sheets went to the press without any assistance, and the rest had the occasional inspection of one or two other friends. If any inaccuracies shall be found in the writing, I shall readily acknowledge them all my own, P. and am, I confess, under no great concern

about them, provided the matter in general
may be found useful and answerable in the
application of it to truth and nature; in which
material points, if the reader shall think fit to
rectify any mistakes, it will give me a sensible
pleasure, and be doing great honour to the
work.

ADVERTISEMENT.

For the more easy finding the figures referred to in the two prints belonging
to this work, the references are for the most part placed at the bottom of
the page. Fig. T. p. 1, signifies the top of plate 1. L. p. 1. the left side. R.
p. 1, the right side. B. p. 1, the bottom. And where a figure is referred to
in the middle of either print, it is only marked thus, fig. p. 1, or fig. p. 2.

INTRODUCTION.

I now offer to the public a short essay, accompanied with two explanatory prints, in which I shall endeavour to show what the principles are in nature by which we are directed to call the forms of some bodies beautiful, others ugly, some graceful, and others the reverse; by considering more minutely than has hitherto been done, the nature of those lines, and their different combinations, which serve to raise in the mind the ideas of all the variety of forms imaginable. At first, perhaps, the whole design, as well as the prints, may seem rather intended to trifle and confound, than to entertain and inform: but I am persuaded that when the examples in nature, referred to in this essay, are duly considered and examined upon the principles laid down in it, it will be thought worthy of a careful and attentive perusal: and the prints themselves too will, I make no doubt, be examined as attentively, when it is found, that almost every figure in them (how oddly soever they may seem to be grouped together) is referred to singly in the essay, in order to assist the reader's imagination, when the original examples in art, or nature, are not themselves before him.

And in this light I hope my prints will be considered, and that the figures referred to in them will never be imagined to be placed there by me as examples themselves of beauty or grace, but only to point out to the reader what sorts of objects he is to look for and examine in nature, or in the works of the greatest masters. My figures, therefore, are to be considered in the same light with those a mathematician makes with his pen, which may convey the idea of his demonstration, though not a line in them is either perfectly straight, or of that peculiar curvature he is treating of. Nay, so far was I from aiming at grace, that I purposely chose to be least accurate where most beauty might be expected, that no stress might be laid on the figures to the prejudice of the work itself : for, I must confess, I have but little hopes of having a favourable attention given to my design in general, by those who have already had a more fashionable introduction into the mysteries of the arts of painting and sculpture. Much less do I expect, or in truth desire, the countenance of that set of people, who have an interest in exploding any kind of doctrine that may teach us to *see with our own eyes.*

It may be needless to observe, that some of the last-mentioned are not only the dependants on, but often the only instructors and leaders of the former ; but in what light they are so con- P. 3 sidered abroad, may be partly seen by * a burlesque representation of them, taken from a. print published by Mr Pond, designed by Cav^r. Ghezzi at Rome.

To those, then, whose judgments are unprejudiced, this little work is submitted with most pleasure ; because it is from such that I have hitherto received the most obligations, and now have reason to expect most candour.

Therefore I would fain have such of my readers be assured, that however they may have been awed and over-born by pompous terms of art, hard names, and the parade of seemingly magnificent collections of pictures and statues, they are in a much fairer way, ladies as well as gentlemen, of gaining a perfect knowledge of the elegant and beautiful, in artificial as well as natural forms, by considering them in a systematical, but, at the same time, familiar way, than those who have been prepossessed by dogmatic rules, taken from the performances of art only : nay, I will venture to say, sooner and more ra-

* Fig. 1. T. p. 1.

tionally than even a tolerable painter, who has imbibed the same prejudices.

The more prevailing the notion may be, that painters and connoisseurs are the only competent judges of things of this sort, the more it becomes necessary to clear up and confirm, as much as possible, what has only been asserted in the foregoing paragraph ; that no one may be deterred, by the want of such previous knowledge, from entering into this enquiry.

4   The reason why gentlemen, who have been inquisitive after knowledge in pictures, have their eyes less qualified for our purpose than others, is because their thoughts have been entirely and continually employed and incumbered with considering and retaining the various *manners* in which pictures are painted, the histories, names, and characters of the masters, together with many other little circumstances belonging to the mechanical part of the art ; and little or no time has been given for perfecting the ideas they ought to have in their minds of the objects themselves in nature : for by having thus espoused and adopted their first notions from nothing but *imitations,* and becoming too often as bigotted to their faults as their beauties, they at length in a manner totally neglect, or at least disregard the works of nature, merely because

they do not tally with what their minds are so strongly prepossessed with.

Were not this a true state of the case, many a reputed capital picture, that now adorns the cabinets of the curious in all countries, would long ago have been committed to the flames: nor would it have been possible for the Venus and Cupid, represented by the figure *, to have made its way into the principal apartment of a palace.

It is also evident that the painter's eye may not be a bit better fitted to receive these new impressions, who is, in like manner, too much captivated with the works of art; for he also is apt to pursue the shadow and drop the substance. This mistake happens chiefly to those who go to Rome for the accomplishment of their studies, as they naturally will, without the utmost care, take the infectious turn of the connoisseur instead of the painter: and in proportion as they turn by those means bad proficients in their own arts, they become the more considerable in that of a connoisseur. As a confirmation of this seeming paradox, it has ever been observed, at all auctions of pictures, that the very worst painters sit as the most profound

* Under fig. 49. T. p. 1.

judges, and are trusted only, I suppose, on account of their *disinterestedness*.

I apprehend a good deal of this will look more like resentment, and a design to invalidate the objections of such as are not likely to set the faults of this work in the most favourable light, than merely for the encouragement, as was said above, of such of my readers as are neither painters nor connoisseurs : and I will be ingenuous enough to confess something of this may be true ; but, at the same time, I cannot allow that this alone would have been a sufficient motive to have made me risk giving offence to any, had not another consideration, besides that already alledged, of more consequence to the purpose in hand, made it necessary. I mean the setting forth, in the strongest colours, the surprising alterations objects seemingly undergo through the prepossessions and prejudices contracted by the mind ;——fallacies strongly to be guarded against by such as would learn to see objects truly !

Although the instances already given are pretty flagrant, yet it is certainly true, (as a farther confirmation of this, and for the consolation of those who may be a little piqued at what has been said,) that painters of every condition are stronger instances of the almost unavoid-

able power of prejudice than any people whatever.

What are all the *manners*, as they are called,
of even the greatest masters, which are known
to differ so much from one another, and all of
them from nature, but so many strong proofs
of their inviolable attachment to falsehood, con-
verted into established truth in their own eyes
by self-opinion? Rubens would, in all probability, have been as much disgusted at the dry
manner of Poussin, as Poussin was at the extravagant of Rubens. The prejudices of inferior
proficients, in favour of the imperfections of their
own performances, is still more amazing.—Their
eyes are so quick in discerning the faults of
others, at the same time they are so totally blind
to their own! Indeed it would be well for us all
if one of Gulliver's flappers could be placed at our
elbows, to remind us at every stroke how much
prejudice and self-opinion perverts our sight.

From what has been said, I hope it appears
that those who have no bias of any kind, either
from their own practice or the lessons of others,
are fittest to examine into the truth of the principles laid down in the following pages. But as
every one may not have had an opportunity of
being sufficiently acquainted with the instances P. 7
that have been given, I will offer one of a familiar kind, which may be a hint for their obser-

ving a thousand more. How gradually does the eye grow reconciled even to a disagreeable dress, as it becomes more and more the fashion, and how soon return to its dislike of it, when it is left off, and a new one has taken possession of the mind!—So vague is taste, when it has no solid principles for its foundation!

Notwithstanding I have told you my design of considering minutely the variety of lines, which serve to raise the ideas of bodies in the mind, and which are undoubtedly to be considered as drawn on the surfaces only of solid or opake bodies; yet the endeavouring to conceive as accurate an idea as is possible of the *inside* of those surfaces, if I may be allowed the expression, will be a great assistance to us in the pursuance of our present enquiry.

In order to my being well understood, let every object under our consideration be imagined to have its inward contents scooped out so nicely as to have nothing of it left but a thin shell, exactly corresponding both in its inner and outer surface to the shape of the object itself: and let us likewise suppose this thin shell to be made up of very fine threads, closely connected together, and equally perceptible, whether the eye is supposed to observe them from without or within, and we shall find the ideas of the two surfaces of this shell will naturally coincide.

The very word, shell, makes us seem to see both surfaces alike.

The use of this conceit, as it may be called P. 8 by some, will be seen to be very great in the process of this work : and the oftener we think of objects in this shell-like manner, we shall facilitate and strengthen our conception of any particular part of the surface of an object we are viewing, by acquiring thereby a more perfect knowledge of the whole, to which it belongs : because the imagination will naturally enter into the vacant space within this shell, and there at once, as from a centre, view the whole form within, and mark the opposite corresponding parts so strongly as to retain the idea of the whole, and make us masters of the meaning of every view of the object, as we walk round it, and view it from without.

Thus the most perfect idea we can possibly acquire of a sphere, is by conceiving an infinite number of straight rays of equal lengths, issuing from the centre, as from the eye, spreading every way alike ; and circumscribed or wound about at their other extremities with close-connected circular threads, or lines, forming a true spherical shell.

But in the common way of taking the view of any opake object, that part of its surface which fronts the eye is apt to occupy the mind

alone, and the opposite, nay, even every other part of it whatever, is left unthought of at that time : and the least motion we make to reconnoitre any other side of the object, confounds our first idea, for want of the connexion of the
P. 9 two ideas, which the complete knowledge of the whole would naturally have given us, if we had considered it in the other way before.

Another advantage of considering objects thus merely as shells composed of lines, is, that by these means we obtain the true and full idea of what is called the *outlines* of a figure, which has been confined within too narrow limits, by taking it only from drawings on paper ; for in the example of the sphere given above, every one of the imaginary circular threads has a right to be considered as an outline of the sphere, as well as those which divide the half that is seen from that which is not seen ; and if the eye be supposed to move regularly round it, these threads will each of them as regularly succeed one another in the office of outlines : (in the narrow and limited sense of the word :) and the instant any one of these threads, during this motion of the eye, comes into sight on one side, its opposite thread is lost, and disappears on the other. He who will thus take the pains of acquiring perfect ideas of the distances, bearings, and oppositions of several material points and lines in the surfaces of even the most irregular figures, will gradually arrive at the knack of recalling them into his mind when the objects themselves are not before him : and they will be as strong and perfect as those of the most plain and regular forms, such as cubes and spheres, and will be of infinite service to those who invent and draw from fancy, as well as enable those to be more correct who draw from the life.

In this manner, therefore, I would desire the P.10 reader to assist his imagination as much as possible, in considering every object, as if his eye were placed within it. As straight lines are easily conceived, the difficulty of following this method in the most simple and regular forms will be less than may be first imagined ; and its use in the more compounded will be greater, as will be more fully shown when we come to speak of composition.

But as fig. * may be of singular use to young designers in the study of the human form, the most complex and beautiful of all, in shewing them a mechanical way of gaining the opposite points in its surface, which never can be seen in one and the same view, it will be proper to explain the design of it in this place, as it may

* Fig. 2. L. p. 1.

at the same time add some weight to what has been already said.

It represents the trunk of a figure cast in soft wax, with one wire passed perpendicularly through its centre, another perpendicularly to the first, going in before and coming out in the middle of the back, and as many more as may be thought necessary, parallel to and at equal distances from these, and each other, as is marked by the several dots in the figure.——Let these wires be so loose as to be taken out at pleasure, but not before all the parts of them, which appear out of the wax, are carefully painted, close up to the wax, of a different co-lour from those that lie within it. By these P. 11 means the horizontal and perpendicular *contents* of these parts of the body (by which I mean the distances of opposite points in the surface of these parts) through which the wires have passed, may be exactly known and compared with each other; and the little holes, where the wires have pierced the wax remaining on its surface, will mark out the corresponding opposite points on the external muscles of the body, as well as as-sist and guide us to a readier conception of all the intervening parts. These points may be marked upon a marble figure with calipers properly used.

INTRODUCTION.

The known method, many years made use of, for the more exactly and expeditiously reducing drawings from large pictures, for engravings, or for enlarging designs for painting ceilings and cupolas, (by striking lines perpendicular to each other, so as to make an equal number of squares on the paper designed for the copy, that hath been first made on the original; by which means the situation of every part of the picture is mechanically seen, and easily transferred) may truly be said to be somewhat of the same kind with what has been here proposed, but that one is done upon a flat surface, the other upon a solid; and that the new scheme differs in its application, and may be of a much more useful and extensive nature than the old one.

But it is time now to have done with the introduction; and I shall proceed to consider the fundamental principles, which are generally allowed to give elegance and beauty, when duly P.12 blended together, to compositions of all kinds whatever; and point out to my readers the particular force of each, in those compositions in nature and art which seem most to *please and entertain the eye*, and give that grace and beauty which is the subject of this enquiry. The principles I mean are, FITNESS, VARIETY,

INTRODUCTION.

UNIFORMITY, SIMPLICITY, INTRICACY, and QUANTITY ;——*all which co-operate in the production of beauty, mutually correcting and restraining each other occasionally.*

THE

ANALYSIS OF BEAUTY.

CHAPTER I.

OF FITNESS.

Fitness of the parts to the design for which every
individual thing is formed, either by art or nature, is
first to be considered, as it is of the greatest consequence to the beauty of the whole. This is so evident,
that even the sense of seeing, the great inlet of beauty,
is itself so strongly biassed by it, that if the mind, on
account of this kind of value in a form, esteem it
beautiful, though on all other considerations it be not
so, the eye grows insensible of its want of beauty,
and even begins to be pleased, especially after it has
been a considerable time acquainted with it.

It is well known, on the other hand, that forms of
great elegance often disgust the eye by being improperly applied. Thus twisted columns are undoubtedly
ornamental ; but as they convey an idea of weakness,
they always displease, when they are improperly made

use of as supporters to any thing that is bulky, or appears heavy.

The bulks and proportions of objects are governed by fitness and propriety. It is this that has established the size and proportion of chairs, tables, and all sorts of utensils and furniture. It is this that has fixed the dimensions of pillars, arches, &c. for the support of great weight, and so regulated all the orders in architecture, as well as the sizes of windows and doors, &c. Thus though a building were ever so large, the steps of the stairs, the seats in the windows must be continued of their usual heights, or they would lose their beauty with their fitness: and in ship-building the dimensions of every part are confined and regulated by fitness for sailing. When a vessel sails well, the sailors always call her a beauty; the two ideas have such a connexion!

The general dimensions of the parts of the human body are adapted thus to the uses they are designed for. The trunk is the most capacious on account of the quantity of its contents, and the thigh is larger than the leg, because it has both the leg and foot to move, the leg only the foot, &c.

15   Fitness of parts also constitutes and distinguishes in a great measure the characteristics of objects; as, for example, the race-horse differs as much in quality, or character, from the war-horse, as to its figure, as the Hercules from the Mercury.

The race-horse, having all its parts of such dimensions as best fit the purposes of speed, acquires on that account a consistent character of one sort of beauty. To illustrate this, suppose the beautiful head and

12

gracefully-turned neck of the war-horse were placed on the shoulders of the race-horse, instead of his own awkward straight one, it would disgust and deform, instead of adding beauty, because the judgment would condemn it as unfit.

The Hercules, by Glicon,* hath all its parts finely fitted for the purposes of the utmost strength the texture of the human form will bear. The back, breast, and shoulders have huge bones, and muscles adequate to the supposed active strength of its upper parts; but, as less strength was required for the lower parts, the judicious sculptor, contrary to all modern rule of enlarging every part in proportion, lessened the size of the muscles gradually down towards the feet; and for the same reason made the neck larger in circumference than any part of the head, otherwise the figure would have been burdened with an unnecessary weight, which would have been a drawback from his strength, and, in consequence of that, from its characteristic beauty.

These seeming faults, which show the superior P. anatomical knowledge as well as judgment of the ancients, are not to be found in the leaden imitations of it near Hyde Park. These saturnine geniuses imagined they knew how to correct such apparent *disproportions.*

These few examples may be sufficient to give an idea of what I mean (and would have understood) by the beauty of fitness, or propriety.

* Fig. 3. p. 1. † Fig. 4. p. 1.

CHAPTER II.

OF VARIETY.

How great a share variety has in producing beauty may be seen in the ornamental part of nature.

The shapes and colours of plants, flowers, leaves, the paintings in butterflies' wings, shells, &c. seem of little other intended use than that of entertaining the eye with the pleasure of variety.

All the senses delight in it, and equally are averse to sameness. The ear is as much offended with one even continued note, as the eye is with being fixed to a point, or to the view of a dead wall.

Yet when the eye is glutted with a succession of variety, it finds relief in a certain degree of sameness ; and even plain space becomes agreeable, and, properly introduced and contrasted with variety, adds to it more variety.

P. 17   I mean here, and every where indeed, a composed variety ; for variety uncomposed, and without design, is confusion and deformity.

Observe, that a gradual lessening is a kind of varying that gives beauty. The pyramid diminishing from its basis to its point, and the scroll or voluta gradually lessening to its centre, are beautiful forms. So also objects that only seem to do so, though in fact they do not, have equal beauty ; thus perspective views, and particularly those of buildings, are always pleasing to the eye.

The little ship, between figure 47 and 88, plate 1, supposed moving along the shore even with the eye, might have its top and bottom bounded by two lines at equal distances all the way, as A; but if the ship puts out to sea, these lines at top and bottom would seem to vary and meet each other by degrees, as B, in the point C, which is in the line where the sky and water meet, called the horizon. Thus much of the manner of perspective adding beauty, by seemingly varying otherwise unvaried forms, I thought might be acceptable to those who have not learnt perspective.

CHAPTER III.

OF UNIFORMITY, REGULARITY, OR SYMMETRY.

P.18 It may be imagined that the greatest part of the effects of beauty results from the symmetry of parts in the object which is beautiful; but I am very well persuaded this prevailing notion will soon appear to have little or no foundation.

It may indeed have properties of greater consequence, such as propriety, fitness, and use, and yet but little serve the purposes of pleasing the eye, merely on the score of beauty.

We have, indeed, in our nature a love of imitation from our infancy, and the eye is often entertained, as well as surprised, with mimicry, and delighted with the exactness of counterparts; but then this always gives way to its superior love of variety, and soon grows tiresome.

If the uniformity of figures, parts, or lines, were truly the chief cause of beauty, the more exactly uniform their appearances were kept the more pleasure the eye would receive: but this is so far from being the case, that, when the mind has been once satisfied that the parts answer one another, with so exact an uniformity as to preserve to the whole the character of fitness to stand, to move, to sink, to swim, to fly, &c. without losing the balance, the eye

is rejoiced to see the object turned, and shifted, so P. 19
as to vary these uniform appearances.

Thus the profile of most objects, as well as faces,
are rather more pleasing than their full fronts.

Whence it is clear the pleasure does not arise
from seeing the exact resemblance which one side
bears the other, but from the knowledge that they
do so on account of fitness, with design, and for use.
For when the head of a fine woman is turned a little
to one side, which takes off from the exact similarity of the two halves of the face, and somewhat
reclining, so varying still more from the straight
and parallel lines of a formal front face, it is always looked upon as most pleasing. This is accordingly said to be a graceful air of the head.

It is a constant rule in composition in painting to
avoid regularity. When we view a building, or any
other object in life, we have it in our power, by shifting the ground, to take that view of it which pleases
us best; and in consequence of this, the painter, if he
is left to his choice, takes it on the angle rather than
in front, as most agreeable to the eye, because the
regularity of the lines is taken away by their running
into perspective, without losing the idea of fitness :
and when he is of necessity obliged to give the front
of a building, with all its equalities and parallelisms,
he generally breaks (as it is termed) such disagreeable
appearances, by throwing a tree before it, or the
shadow of an imaginary cloud, or some other object P. 20
that may answer the same purpose of adding variety,
which is the same with taking away uniformity.

If uniform objects were agreeable, why is there

properly made such care taken to contrast and vary all the limbs of a statue ?

The picture of Henry the Eighth * would be preferable to the finely contrasted figures of Guido or Correggio ; and the Antinous's easy sway † must submit to the stiff and straight figure of the dancing-master ; ‡ and the uniform outlines of the muscles in the figure § taken from Albert Durar's book of proportions, would have more taste in them than those in the famous part of an antique ‖ figure from which Michael Angelo acquired so much of his skill in grace.

In short, whatever appears to be fit, and proper to answer great purposes, ever satisfies the mind, and pleases on that account. Uniformity is of this kind. We find it necessary, in some degree, to give the idea of rest and motion without the possibility of falling. But when any such purposes can be as well effected by more irregular parts, the eye is always better pleased on the account of variety.

How pleasingly is the idea of firmness in standing conveyed to the eye by the three elegant claws of a table, the three feet of a tea-lamp, or the celebrated tripod of the ancients ?

Thus you see regularity, uniformity, or symmetry, please only as they serve to give the idea of fitness.

* Fig. 72. p. 2.　　† Fig. 6. p. 1.　　‡ Fig. 7. p. 1.
§ Fig. 55. p. 1.　　‖ Fig. 54.

CHAPTER IV.

OF SIMPLICITY, OR DISTINCTNESS.

SIMPLICITY, without variety, is wholly insipid, and P. 21 at best does only not displease; but when variety is joined to it then it pleases, because it enhances the pleasure of variety, by giving the eye the power of enjoying it with ease.

There is no object composed of straight lines that has so much variety, with so few parts, as the pyramid: and it is its constantly varying from its base gradually upwards in every situation of the eye, (without giving the idea of sameness, as the eye moves round it) that has made it be esteemed in all ages, in preference to the cone, which in all views appears nearly the same, being varied only by light and shade.

Steeples, monuments, and most compositions in painting and sculpture, are kept within the form of the cone or pyramid, as the most eligible boundary on account of their simplicity and variety. For the same reason equestrian statues please more than the single figures.

The authors (for there were three concerned in the work) of as fine a group of figures in sculpture as ever was made either by ancients or moderns, (I mean Laocoon and his two sons) chose to be guilty of the absurdity of making the sons of half the father's size, though they have every other mark of being de- P. 22

signed for men, rather than not bring their composition within the boundary of a pyramid.* Thus, if a judicious workman were employed to make a case of wood, for preserving it from the injuries of the weather, or for the convenience of carriage, he would soon find, by his eye, the whole composition would readily fit, and be easily packed up, in one of a pyramidal form.

Steeples, &c. have generally been varied from the cone, to take off from their too great simplicity, and instead of their circular bases, polygons of different, but even numbers of sides, have been substituted, I suppose for the sake of uniformity. These forms, however, may be said to have been chosen by the architect with a view to the cone, as the whole composition might be bounded by it.

Yet, in my mind, odd numbers have the advantage over the even ones, as variety is more pleasing than uniformity, where the same end is answered by both, as in this case, where both polygons may be circumscribed by the same circle, or, in other words, both compositions bounded by the same cone.

And I cannot help observing, that Nature, in all her works of fancy, if I may be allowed the expression, where it seems immaterial whether even or odd numbers of divisions were preferred, most frequently employs the odd; as, for example, in the indenting of leaves, flowers, blossoms, &c.

P.23   The oval also, on account of its variety with simplicity, is as much to be preferred to the circle, as the

* Fig. 9. T. p. 1.

triangle to the square, or the pyramid to the cube; and this figure lessened at one end, like the egg, thereby being more varied, is singled out by the author of all variety, to bound the features of a beautiful face.

When the oval has a little more of the cone added to it than the egg has, it becomes more distinctly a compound of those two most simple varied figures. This is the shape of the pine-apple,* which nature has particularly distinguished by bestowing ornaments of rich mosaic upon it, composed of contrasted serpentine lines, and the pips,† as the gardeners call them, are still varied by two cavities and one round eminence in each.

Could a more elegant simple form than this have been found, it is probable that judicious architect, Sir Christopher Wren, would not have chosen the pine-apples for the two terminations of the sides of the front of St Paul's: and perhaps the globe and cross, though a finely varied figure, which terminates the dome, would not have had the preference of situation, if a religious motive had not been the occasion.

Thus we see simplicity gives beauty even to variety, as it makes it more easily understood, and should be ever studied in the works of art, as it serves to prevent perplexity in forms of elegance; as will be shewn in the next chapter.

* Fig. 10. p. 1.   † Fig. 11. T. p. 1.

CHAPTER V.

OF INTRICACY.

P. 24 THE active mind is ever bent to be employed. Pursuing is the business of our lives ; and, even abstracted from any other view, gives pleasure. Every arising difficulty, that for a while attends and interrupts the pursuit, gives a sort of spring to the mind, enhances the pleasure, and makes what would else be toil and labour, become sport and recreation.

Wherein would consist the joys of hunting, shooting, fishing, and many other favourite diversions, without the frequent turns and difficulties, and disappointments, that are daily met with in the pursuit? —how joyless does the sportsman return when the hare has not had fair play ! how lively, and in spirits, even when an old cunning one has baffled and outrun the dogs !

This love of pursuit, merely as pursuit, is implanted in our natures, and designed, no doubt, for necessary and useful purposes. Animals have it evidently by instinct. The hound dislikes the game he so eagerly pursues ; and even cats will risk the losing of their prey to chase it over again. It is a pleasing labour of the mind to solve the most difficult problems; allegories and riddles, trifling as they are, afford the mind amusement : and with what delight does it follow the well-connected thread of a play, or novel, which ever increases as the plot thickens, and ends most pleased P. 25 when that is most distinctly unravelled !

The eye hath this sort of enjoyment in winding walks, and serpentine rivers, and all sorts of objects, whose forms, as we shall see hereafter, are composed principally of what I call the *waving* and *serpentine* lines.

Intricacy in form, therefore, I shall define to be that peculiarity in the lines, which compose it, that *leads the eye a wanton kind of chase,* and from the pleasure that gives the mind, intitles it to the name of beautiful: and it may be justly said, that the cause of the idea of grace more immediately resides in this principle than in the other five, except variety; which indeed includes this and all the others.

That this observation may appear to have a real foundation in nature, every help will be required which the reader himself can call to his assistance, as well as what will here be suggested to him.

To set this matter in somewhat a clearer light, the familiar instance of a common jack, with a circular fly, may serve our purpose better than a more elegant form: preparatory to which let the figure * be considered, which represents the eye, at a common reading distance viewing a row of letters, but fixed with most attention to the middle letter A.

Now as we read, a ray may be supposed to be drawn from the centre of the eye to that letter it looks at first, and to move successively with it from P. 26 letter to letter, the whole length of the line: but if

* Fig. 14. T. p. 1.

the eye stops at any particular letter, A, to observe it more than the rest, these other letters will grow more and more imperfect to the sight the farther they are situated on either side of A, as is expressed in the figure : and when we endeavour to see all the letters in a line equally perfect at one view, as it were, this imaginary ray must course it to and fro with great celerity. Thus though the eye, strictly speaking, can only pay due attention to these letters in succession, yet the amazing ease and swiftness with which it performs this task, enables us to see considerable spaces with sufficient satisfaction at one sudden view.

Hence we shall always suppose some such principal ray moving along with the eye, and tracing out the parts of every form we mean to examine in the most perfect manner : and when we would follow with exactness the course any body takes that is in motion, this ray is always to be supposed to move with the body.

In this manner of attending to forms they will be found, whether at *rest* or in *motion*, to give *movement* to this imaginary ray ; or, more properly speaking, to the eye itself, affecting it *thereby* more or less *pleasingly*, according to their different *shapes* and *motions.* Thus, for example, in the instance of the jack, whether the eye (with this imaginary ray) P. 27 moves slowly down the line, to which the weight is fixed, or attends to the slow motion of the weight itself, the mind is equally fatigued : and whether it swiftly courses round the circular rim of the flyer, when the jack stands, or nimbly follows one point in its circularity whilst it is whirling about, we are almost equally made giddy by it. But our sensation differs much from either of these unpleasant ones when we observe the curling worm, into which the worm-wheel is fixed: * for this is always pleasing, either at rest or in motion, and whether that motion is slow or quick.

That it is accounted so, when it is *at rest*, appears by the ribbon, twisted round a stick, (represented on one side of this figure,) which has been a long-established ornament in the carvings of frames, chimney-pieces, and door-cases, and called by the carvers *the stick and ribbon ornament;* and when the stick through the middle is omitted, it is called the *ribbon edge;* both to be seen in almost every house of fashion.

But the pleasure it gives the eye is still more lively when *in motion.* I never can forget my frequent strong attention to it when I was very young, and that its beguiling movement gave me the same kind of sensation then which I since have felt at seeing a country-dance, though perhaps the latter might be somewhat more engaging, particularly when my eye eagerly pursued a favourite dancer through all the windings of the figure, who then was bewitching to the sight, as the imaginary ray we were speaking of P. 28 was dancing with her all the time.

This single example might be sufficient to explain what I mean by *the beauty of a composed intricacy of form*, and how it may be said, with propriety, to *lead* the eye a *kind of chase.*

* Fig. 15. T. p. 1.

But the hair of the head is another very obvious instance, which, being designed chiefly as an ornament, proves more or less so according to the form it naturally takes, or is put into by art. The most amiable in itself is the flowing curl; and the many waving and contrasted turns of naturally intermingling locks ravish the eye with the pleasure of the pursuit, especially when they are put in motion by a gentle breeze. The poet knows it as well as the painter, and has described the wanton ringlets waving in the wind.

And yet to shew how excess ought to be avoided in intricacy, as well as in every other principle, the very same head of hair, whisped and matted together, would make the most disagreeable figure; because the eye would be perplexed, and at a fault, and unable to trace such a confused number of uncomposed and entangled lines; and yet, notwithstanding this, the present fashion the ladies have gone into, of wearing a part of the hair of their heads braided together from behind, like intertwisted serpents, arising thickest from the bottom, lessening as it is P. 29 brought forward, and naturally conforming to the shape of the rest of the hair it is pinned over, is extremely picturesque. Their thus interlacing the hair in distinct varied quantities is an artful way of preserving as much of intricacy as is beautiful.

CHAPTER VI.

OF QUANTITY.

FORMS of magnitude, although ill-shaped, will however, on account of their vastness, draw our attention and raise our admiration.

Huge shapeless rocks have a pleasing kind of horror in them, and the wide ocean awes us with its vast contents; but when forms of beauty are presented to the eye in large quantities, the pleasure increases on the mind, and horror is softened into reverence.

How solemn and pleasing are groves of high-grown trees, great churches, and palaces? has not even a single spreading oak, grown to maturity, acquired the character of the venerable oak?

Windsor castle is a noble instance of the effect of quantity. The hugeness of its few distinct parts strikes the eye with uncommon grandeur at a distance, as well as nigh. It is quantity, with simplicity, which makes it one of the finest objects in the kingdom, though void of any regular order of architecture.

The Façade of the old Louvre at Paris is also remarkable for its quantity. This fragment is allowed to be the finest piece of building in France, though there are many equal, if not superior, to it in all other respects except that of quantity.

Who does not feel a pleasure when he pictures in his mind the immense buildings which once adorned the lower Egypt, by imagining the whole complete, and ornamented with colossal statues?

Elephants and whales please us with their unwieldy greatness. Even large personages, merely for being so, command respect: nay, quantity is an addition to the person which often supplies a deficiency in his figure.

The robes of state are always made large and full, because they give a grandeur of appearance, suitable to the offices of the greatest distinction. The judge's robes have an awful dignity given them by the quantity of their contents; and, when the train is held up, there is a noble waving line descending from the shoulders of the judge to the hand of his train-bearer. So, when the train is gently thrown aside, it generally falls into a great variety of folds, which again employ the eye, and fix its attention.

The grandeur of the Eastern dress, which so far surpasses the European, depends as much on quantity as on costliness.

In a word, it is quantity which adds greatness to grace. But then excess is to be avoided, or quantity will become clumsy, heavy, or ridiculous.

P. 31   The full-bottom wig, like the lion's mane, hath something noble in it, and adds not only dignity, but sagacity to the countenance: * but were it to be worn as large again, it would become a burlesque; or was an improper person to put it on, it would then too be ridiculous.

When improper, or *incompatible* excesses meet, they always excite laughter; more especially when

* Fig. 16. p. 1.

the forms of those excesses are inelegant, that is, when they are composed of unvaried lines.

For example, the figure referred to in the margin,* represents a fat grown face of a man, with an infant's cap on, and the rest of the child's dress stuffed, and so well placed under his chin, as to seem to belong to that face. This is a contrivance I have seen at Bartholomew-fair, and always occasioned a roar of laughter. The next † is of the same kind, a child with a man's wig and cap on. In these you see the ideas of youth and age jumbled together in forms without beauty.

- So a Roman general, ‡ dressed by a modern tailor and peruke-maker for tragedy, is a comic figure.—— The dresses of the times are mixed, and the lines which compose them are straight or only round.

Dancing-masters, representing deities in their grand ballets on the stage, are no less ridiculous. See the Jupiter.§

Nevertheless custom and fashion will, in length of time, reconcile almost every absurdity whatever to the eye, or make it overlooked.

It is from the same joining of opposite ideas that P. 32 makes us laugh at the owl and the ass, for under their awkward forms they seem to be gravely musing and meditating, as if they had the sense of human beings.

A monkey too, whose figure, as well as most of

* Fig. 17. T. p. 1.   † Fig. 18. T. p. 1.   ‡ Fig. 19. T. p. 1.
§ Fig. 20. T. p. 1.

his actions, so oddly resembles the human, is also very comical; and he becomes more so when a coat is put on him, as he then becomes a greater burlesque on the man.

There is something extremely odd and comical in the rough shock dog. The ideas here connected are the inelegant and inanimate figure of a thrum mop, or muff, and that of a sensible, friendly animal, which is as much a burlesque of the dog, as the monkey when his coat is on is of the man.

What can it be but this inelegance of the figure, joined with impropriety, that makes a whole audience burst into laughter when they see the miller's sack, in Dr Faustus, jumping cross the stage? Was a well-shaped vase to do the same, it would equally surprise, but not make every body laugh, because the elegance of the form would prevent it.

For when the forms, thus joined together, are each of them elegant, and composed of agreeable lines, they will be so far from making us laugh, that they will become entertaining to the imagination, as well as pleasing to the eye. The sphinx and siren have been admired and accounted ornamental in all ages. P. 33 The former represents strength and beauty joined; the latter, beauty and swiftness in pleasing and graceful forms.

The griffin, a modern hieroglyphic, signifying strength and swiftness, united in the two noble forms of the lion and eagle, is a grand object. So the antique centaur hath a savage greatness as well as beauty.

These may be said to be monsters, it's true; but

then they convey such noble ideas, and have such elegance in their forms, as greatly compensates for their being unnaturally joined together.

I shall mention but one more instance of this sort, and that the most extraordinary of all, which is an infant's head of about two years old, with a pair of duck's wings placed under its chin, supposed always to be flying about and singing psalms.*

A painter's representation of heaven would be nothing without swarms of these little inconsistent objects flying about, or perching on the clouds; and yet there is something so agreeable in their form, that the eye is reconciled and overlooks the absurdity, and we find them in the carving and painting of almost every church. St Paul's is full of them.

As the foregoing principles are the very groundwork of what is to follow, we will, in order to make them the more familiar to us, just speak of them in the way they are daily put in practice, and may be seen in every dress that is worn; and we shall find not only that ladies of fashion, but that women of every rank who are said to dress prettily, have known their force, without considering them as principles. P. 34

Fitness is first considered by them, as knowing that their dresses should be useful, commodious, and fitted to their different ages; or rich, airy, and loose, agreeable to the character they would give out to the public by their dress.

II. Uniformity is chiefly complied with in dress on account of fitness, and seems to be extended not

---

* Fig. 22. R. p. 1.

much farther than dressing both arms alike, and having the shoes of the same colour. For when any part of dress has not the excuse of fitness or propriety for its uniformity of parts, the ladies always call it *formal.*

For which reason, when they are at liberty to make what shapes they please in ornamenting their persons, those of the best taste chuse the irregular as the more engaging ; for example, no two patches are ever chosen of the same size, or placed at the same height ; nor a single one in the middle of a feature, unless it be to hide a blemish ; so a single feather, flower, or jewel is generally placed on one side of the head ; or, if ever put in front, it is turned awry to avoid formality.

It was once the fashion to have two curls of equal size, stuck at the same height close upon the forehead, which probably took its rise from seeing the pretty effect of curls falling loosely over the face.

A lock of hair falling thus cross the temples, and by that means breaking the regularity of the oval, has an effect too alluring to be strictly decent, as is very well known to the loose and lowest class of women : but being paired in so stiff a manner as they formerly were, they lost the desired effect, and ill deserved the name of favourites.

III. Variety in dress, both as to colour and form, is the constant study of the young and gay—But then,

IV. That taudriness may not destroy the proper effect of variety, simplicity is called in to restrain its superfluities, and is often very artfully made use of to set native beauty off to more advantage. I have not known any set of people that have more excelled in this principle of simplicity, or plainness, than the Quakers.

V. Quantity, or fulness in dress, has ever been a darling principle; so that sometimes those parts of dress which would properly admit of being extended to a great degree, have been carried into such strange excesses, that in the reign of Queen Elizabeth a law was made to put a stop to the growth of ruffs: nor is the enormous size of the hoops at present a less sufficient proof of the extraordinary love of quantity P. 36 in dress beyond that of convenience or elegance.

VI. The beauty of intricacy lies in contriving winding shapes, such as the antique lappets belonging to the head of the sphinx,* or as the modern lappet when it is brought before. Every part of dress that will admit of the application of this principle, has an air (as it is termed) given to it thereby; and although it requires dexterity and a taste to execute these windings well, we find them daily practised with success.

This principle also recommends modesty in dress to keep up our expectations, and not suffer them to be too soon gratified. Therefore the body and limbs should all be covered, and little more than certain hints be given of them through the cloathing.

The face indeed will bear a constant view, yet always entertain and keep our curiosity awake without the assistance either of a mask or veil; because

* Fig. 21. p. 1.

vast variety of changing circumstances keeps the eye and the mind in constant play, in following the numberless turns of expression it is capable of. How soon does a face that wants expression grow insipid, though it be ever so pretty!—The rest of the body, not having these advantages in common with the face, would soon satiate the eye, were it to be as constantly exposed, nor would it have more effect than a marble statue. But when it is artfully cloath-
P. 37 ed and decorated, the mind at every turn resumes its imaginary pursuits concerning it. Thus, if I may be allowed a simile, the angler chooses not to see the fish he angles for until it is fairly caught.

CHAPTER VII.

OF LINES.

It may be remembered, that, in the introduction, the reader is desired to consider the surfaces of objects as so many shells of lines, closely connected together, which idea of them it will now be proper to call to mind, for the better comprehending not only this, but all the following chapters on composition.

The constant use made of lines by mathematicians as well as painters, in describing things upon paper, hath established a conception of them, as if actually existing on the real forms themselves. This likewise we suppose, and shall set out with saying, in general, That *the straight line* and *the circular line*, together with their different combinations, and variations, &c. bound and circumscribe all visible objects whatsoever, thereby producing such endless variety of forms as lays us under the necessity of dividing and distinguishing them into general classes, leaving the intervening mixtures of appearances to the reader's own farther observation.

First, * objects composed of straight lines only, as the cube; or of circular lines, as the sphere; or of both together, as cylinders and cones, &c.

Secondly, † those composed of straight lines, cir- P. 38

* Fig. 23. T. p. 1.   † Fig. 24. T. p. 1.

cular lines, and of lines partly straight and partly circular, as the capitals of columns and vases, &c.

Thirdly,* those composed of all the former together, with an addition of the waving line, which is a line more productive of beauty than any of the former, as in flowers, and other forms of the ornamental kind : for which reason we shall call it the line of beauty.

Fourthly,† those composed of all the former together with the serpentine line, as the human form, which line hath the power of superadding grace to beauty. Note,—Forms of most grace have least of the straight line in them.

It is to be observed, that straight lines vary only in length, and therefore are least ornamental.

That curved lines, as they can be varied in their degrees of curvature as well as in their lengths, begin on that account to be ornamental.

That straight and curved lines joined, being a compound line, vary more than curves alone, and so become somewhat more ornamental.

That the waving line, or line of beauty, varying still more, being composed of two curves contrasted, becomes still more ornamental and pleasing, insomuch that the hand takes a lively movement in making it with pen or pencil.

And that the serpentine line, by its waving and winding at the same time different ways, leads the eye in a pleasing manner along the continuity of its
P. 39 variety, if I may be allowed the expression ; and which, by its twisting so many different ways, may

* Fig. 25. T. p. 1.   † Fig. 26. T. p. 1.

be said to inclose (though but a single line) varied contents; and therefore all its variety cannot be expressed on paper by one continued line, without the assistance of the imagination, or the help of a figure; see * where that sort of proportioned winding line, which will hereafter be called the precise serpentine line, or *line of grace*, is represented by a fine wire, properly twisted round the elegant and varied figure of a cone.

* Fig. 26. T. p. 1.

CHAPTER VIII.

OF WHAT SORT OF PARTS, AND HOW PLEASING FORMS ARE COMPOSED.

THUS far having endeavoured to open as large an idea as possible of the power of variety, by having partly shewn that those lines which have most variety in themselves contribute most towards the production of beauty, we will next show how lines may be put together, so as to make pleasing figures or compositions.

In order to be as clear as possible, we will give a few examples of the most familiar and easy sort, and let them serve as a clue to be pursued in the imagination; I say in the imagination chiefly, for the following method is not meant always to be put in practice, or followed in every case, for indeed that could hardly be, and in some it would be ridiculously losing time if it could—Yet there may be cases where it may be necessary to follow this method minutely; as, for example, in architecture.

I am thoroughly convinced in myself, however it may startle some, that a completely new and harmonious order of architecture in all its parts might be produced by the following method of composing, but hardly with certainty without it; and this I am the more apt to believe, as, upon the strictest exa-

P. 40

mination, those four orders of the ancients, which are so well established for beauty and true proportion, perfectly agree with the scheme we shall now lay down.

This way of composing pleasing forms, is to be accomplished by making choice of variety of lines as to their shapes and dimensions ; and then again by varying their situations with each other, by all the different ways that can be conceived : and at the same time (if a solid figure be the subject of the composition) the contents, or space that is to be inclosed within those lines, must be duly considered and varied too, as much as possible, with propriety. In a word, it may be said the art of composing well is the art of varying well. It is not expected that this should at first be perfectly comprehended, yet I believe it will be made sufficiently clear by the help of the examples following :

The figure * represents the simple and pleasing figure of a bell ; this shell, as we may call it, is composed of waving lines, encompassing or bounding P. 41 within it the varied space marked with dotted lines ; here you see the variety of the space within is equal to the beauty of its form without ; and if the space or contents were to be more varied, the outward form would have still more beauty.

As a proof, see a composition of more parts, and a way by which those parts may be put together by a certain method of varying ; i. e. how the one half of

* Fig. 29. T. p. I.

the socket of the candlestick A,* may be varied as the other half B.   Let a convenient and fit height be first given for a candlestick, as †, then let the necessary size of the socket be determined as at (a),‡ after which, in order to give it a better form, let every *distance* or length of divisions differ from the length of the socket, as also vary in their distances from each other, as is seen by the points on the line under the socket (a) ; that is, let any two points, *signifying distance*, be placed farthest from any other two near points, observing always that there should be one distance or part larger than all the rest, and you will readily see that variety could not be so complete without it.—In like manner, let the horizontal distances (always keeping within the bounds of fitness) be varied both as to distances and situations, as on the opposite side of the same figure (b) ; then unite and join all the several distances into a complete shell, by applying several parts of curves and straight lines ; varying them also by making them of different sizes, as (c) : and apply them as at (d) in the same figure, and you have the candlestick, § and with still more variations on the other side.   If you divide the candlestick into many more parts it will appear crowded, as ‖ it will want distinctness of form on a near view, and lose the effect of variety at a distance : this the eye will easily distinguish on removing pretty far from it.

P. 42

Simplicity in composition, or distinctness of parts,

* Fig. 30. T. p. 1.   † Fig. 31. T. p. 1.   ‡ Fig. 32.
          § Fig. 33. T. p. 1.   ‖ Fig. 34. T. p. 1.

is ever to be attended to, as it is one part of beauty, as has been already said; but that what I mean by distinctness of parts in this place may be better understood, it will be proper to explain it by an example.

When you would compose an object of a great variety of parts, let several of those parts be distinguished by themselves by their remarkable difference from the next adjoining, so as to make each of them as it were one well-shaped quantity or part, as is marked by the dotted lines in figure* (these are like what they call passages in music, and in writing paragraphs) by which means not only the whole, but even every part, will be better understood by the eye; for confusion will hereby be avoided when the object is seen near, and the shapes will seem well varied, though fewer in number, at a distance; as figure †, supposed to be the same as the former, but removed so far off that the eye loses sight of the smaller members.

The parsley-leaf, ‡ in like manner, from whence a beautiful foliage in ornament was originally taken, is divided into three distinct passages, which are again divided into other odd numbers; and this method is observed, for the generality, in the leaves of all plants and flowers, the most simple of which are the trefoil and cinquefoil. P.

Light and shade, and colours, also must have their distinctness to make objects completely beautiful; but of these in their proper places—only I will give you a general idea of what is here meant by the

* Fig. 35. T. p. 1.   † Fig. 36. T. p. 1.   ‡ Fig. 37. T. p. 1.

beauty of distinctness of forms, lights, shades, and colours, by putting you in mind of the reverse effects in all them together.

Observe the well-composed nosegay how it loses all its distinctness when it dies; each leaf and flower then shrivels and loses its distinct shape, and the firm colours fade into a kind of sameness; so that the whole gradually becomes a confused heap.

If the general parts of objects are preserved large at first, they will always admit of farther enrichments of a small kind, but then they must be so small as not to confound the general masses or quantities.—Thus you see variety is a check upon itself when overdone, which of course begets what is called a *petit taste* and a confusion to the eye.

It will not be amiss next to show what effects an object or two will have that are put together without, or contrary to these rules of composing variety. Figure * is taken from one of those branches fixed to the sides of common old-fashioned stove-grates by way of ornament, wherein you see how the parts have been varied by fancy only, and yet pretty well: close to which † is another, with about the like number of parts; but as the shapes neither are enough varied as to their contents, nor in their situations with each other, but one shape follows its exact likeness, it is therefore a disagreeable and tasteless figure, and for the same reason the candlestick, fig. ‡ is still worse, as there is less variety in it. Nay, it

P. 44

* Fig. 38. L. p. 1.   † Fig. 39. L. p. 1.   ‡ Fig. 40. T. p. 1.

1

would be better to be quite plain, as figure*, than with such poor attempts at ornament.

These few examples, well understood, will, I imagine, be sufficient to put what was said at the beginning of this chapter out of all doubt, viz. that *the art of composing well* is no more than the *art of varying well;* and to shew, that the method which has been here explained must consequently produce a pleasing proportion amongst the parts, as well as that all deviations from it will produce the contrary. Yet to strengthen this latter assertion, let the following figures, taken from the life, be examined by the above rules for composing, and it will be found that the Indian-fig, or torch-thistle, figure†, as well as all that tribe of uncouth-shaped exotics, have the same reasons for being ugly as the candlestick, fig. 40; as also that the beauties of the Lily ‡ and the calcidonian Iris § proceed from their being composed with great variety, and that the loss of variety, to a certain degree, in the imitations of those flowers underneath them, (fig. 45 and 46,) is the cause of the meanness of their shapes, though they retain enough to be called by the same names.

Hitherto, with regard to composition, little else P. 45 but forms made up of straight and curved lines have been spoken of, and though these lines have but little variety in themselves, yet by reason of the great diversifications that they are capable of in being joined with one another, great variety of beauty of the more useful sort is produced by them

---

* Fig. 41. T. p. 1.   † Fig. 42. T. p. 1.   ‡ Fig. 43. T. p. 1.
§ Fig. 44. T. p. 1.

as in necessary utensils and building: but, in my opinion, buildings, as I before hinted, might be much more varied than they are, for after *fitness* hath been strictly and mechanically complied with, any additional ornamental members, or parts, may, by the foregoing rules, be varied with equal elegance; nor can I help thinking but that churches, palaces, hospitals, prisons, common houses, and summer-houses, might be built more in distinct characters than they are, by contriving orders suitable to each; whereas were a modern architect to build a palace in Lapland or the West Indies, Paladio must be his guide, nor would he dare to stir a step without his book.

Have not many Gothic buildings a great deal of consistent beauty in them? perhaps acquired by a series of improvements made from time to time by the natural persuasion of the eye, which often very near answers the end of working by principles, and sometimes begets them. There is at present such a thirst after variety, that even paltry imitations of Chinese buildings have a kind of vogue, chiefly on account of their novelty: but not only these, but any other new-invented characters of building might P. 46 be regulated by proper principles. The mere ornaments of building, to be sure, at least might be allowed a greater latitude than they are at present; as capitals, frizes, &c. in order to increase the beauty of variety.

Nature, in shells and flowers, &c. affords an infinite choice of elegant hints for this purpose; as the original of the Corinthian capital was taken from nothing more, as is said, than some dock-leaves growing up against a basket. Even a capital composed of the awkward and confined forms of hats and periwigs, as fig. *, in a skilful hand might be made to have some beauty.

However, though the moderns have not made many additions to the art of building, with respect to mere beauty or ornament, yet, it must be confessed, they have carried simplicity, convenience, and neatness of workmanship to a very great degree of perfection, particularly in England, where plain good sense hath preferred these more necessary parts of beauty, which every body can understand, to that richness of taste which is so much to be seen in other countries, and so often substituted in their room.

St Paul's cathedral is one of the noblest instances that can be produced of the most judicious application of every principle that has been spoken of. There you may see the utmost variety without confusion, simplicity without nakedness, richness without taudriness, distinctness without hardness, and quantity without excess. Whence the eye is entertained P. throughout with the charming variety of all its parts together; the noble projecting quantity of a certain number of them, which presents bold and distinct parts at a distance, when the lesser parts within them disappear; and the grand few, but remarkably well-varied parts that continue to please the eye as long as the object is discernible, are evident proofs of the superior skill of Sir Christopher Wren, so justly esteemed the prince of architects.

* Fig. 48. p. 1.
12

It will scarcely admit of a dispute, that the outside of this building is much more perfect than that of St Peter's at Rome : but the inside, though as fine and noble as the space it stands on, and our religion will allow of, must give way to the splendour, shew, and magnificence of that of St Peter's, on account of the sculptures and paintings, as well as the greater magnitude of the whole, which makes it excel as to quantity.

There are many other churches of great beauty, the work of the same architect, which are hid in the heart of the city, whose steeples and spires are raised higher than ordinary, that they may be seen at a distance above the other buildings ; and the great number of them dispersed about the whole city, adorn the prospect of it, and give an air of opulency and magnificence : on which account their shapes will be found to be particularly beautiful. Of these, and perhaps of any in Europe, St Mary-le-bow is the most elegantly varied. St Bride's in Fleet-street diminishes sweetly by elegant degrees, but its variations, though very curious when you are near them, not being quite so bold and distinct as those of Bow, it too soon loses variety at a distance. Some Gothic spires are finely and artfully varied, particularly the famous steeple of Strasburg.

Westminster-Abbey is a good contrast to St Paul's with regard to simplicity and distinctness, the great number of its filligrean ornaments, and small divided and subdivided parts, appear confused when nigh, and are totally lost at a moderate distance ; yet there is nevertheless such a consistency of parts altogether

in a good Gothic taste, and such propriety relative
to the gloomy ideas they were then calculated to
convey, that they have at length acquired an established and distinct character in building. It would
be looked upon as an impropriety, and as a kind of
profanation, to build places for mirth and entertainment in the same taste.

CHAPTER IX.

OF COMPOSITION WITH THE WAVING-LINE.

THERE is scarce a room in any house whatever where one does not see the waving-line employed in some way or other. How inelegant would the shapes of all our moveables be without it ! how very plain and unornamental the mouldings of cornices and chimney-pieces without the variety introduced by the *ogee* member, which is entirely composed of waving-lines !

49   Though all sorts of waving-lines are ornamental, when properly applied, yet, strictly speaking, there is but one precise line properly to be called the line of *beauty*, which in the scale of them * is number 4 : the lines 5, 6, 7, by their bulging too much in their curvature, becoming gross and clumsy ; and, on the contrary, 3, 2, 1, as they straighten, becoming mean and poor, as will appear in the next figure†, where they are applied to the legs of chairs.

A still more perfect idea of the effects of the precise waving-line, and of those lines that deviate from it, may be conceived by the row of stays, figure ‡, where number 4 is composed of precise waving-lines,

* Fig. 49. T. p. 1.   † Fig. 50. T. p. 1.   ‡ Fig. 53. B. p. 1.

and is therefore the best shaped stay. Every whalebone of a good stay must be made to bend in this manner; for the whole stay, when put close together behind, is truly a shell of well-varied contents, and its surface of course a fine form ; so that if a line, or the lace were to be drawn, or brought from the top of the lacing of the stay behind, round the body and down to the bottom peak of the stomacher, it would form such a perfect precise serpentine-line as has been shewn, round the cone, figure 26 in plate 1.—— For this reason all ornaments obliquely contrasting the body in this manner, as the ribbons worn by the knights of the garter, are both genteel and graceful. The numbers 5, 6, 7, and 3, 2. 1, are deviations into stiffness and meanness on one hand, and clumsiness and deformity on the other. The reasons for which P. 50 disagreeable effects, after what has been already said, will be evident to the meanest capacity.

It may be worth our notice, however, that the stay, number 2, would better fit a well-shaped man than number 4 ; and that number 4 would better fit a well-formed woman than number 2 ; and when, on considering them merely as to their forms, and comparing them together as you would do two vases, it has been shown by our principles how much finer and more beautiful number 4 is than number 2, does not this our determination enhance the merit of these principles, as it proves at the same time how much the form of a woman's body surpasses in beauty that of a man ?

From the examples that have been given, enough may be gathered to carry on our observations from them to any other objects that may chance to come in our way, either animate or inanimate, so that we may not only *lineally* account for the ugliness of the toad, the hog, the bear, and the spider, which are totally void of this waving-line, but also for the different degrees of beauty belonging to those objects that possess it.

CHAPTER X.

OF COMPOSITIONS WITH THE SERPENTINE-LINE.

THE very great difficulty there is in describing this line, either in words or by the pencil, (as was hinted before when I first mentioned it,) will make it necessary for me to proceed very slowly in what I have to say in this chapter, and to beg the reader's patience, whilst I lead him, step by step, into the knowledge of what I think the sublime in form, so remarkably displayed in the human body; in which I believe, when he is once acquainted with the idea of them, he will find this species of lines to be principally concerned. P. 51

First, then, let him consider fig. *, which represents a straight horn, with its contents, and he will find, as it varies like the cone, it is a form of some beauty merely on that account.

Next, let him observe in what manner and in what degree the beauty of this horn is increased, in fig. †, where it is supposed to be bent two different ways.

And, lastly, let him attend to the vast increase of beauty, even to grace and elegance, in the same horn, fig. ‡, where it is supposed to have been twisted

* Fig. 56. B. p. 2.   † Fig. 57. B. p. 2.   ‡ Fig. 58. B. p. 2.

round, at the same time that it was bent two different ways, (as in the last figure.)

In the first of these figures, the dotted line down the middle expresses the straight lines of which it is composed ; which, without the assistance of curve lines, or light and shade, would hardly shew it to have contents.

The same is true of the second, though, by the bending of the horn, the straight dotted line is changed into the beautiful waving-line.

52 But in the last, this dotted line, by the twisting as well as the bending of the horn, is changed from the waving into the serpentine-line, which, as it dips out of sight behind the horn in the middle, and returns again at the smaller end, not only gives play to the imagination, and delights the eye on that account, but informs it likewise of the quantity and variety of the contents.

I have chosen this simple example as the easiest way of giving a plain and general idea of the peculiar qualities of these serpentine-lines, and the advantages of bringing them into compositions where the contents you are to express admit of grace and elegance.

And I beg the same things may be understood of these serpentine-lines that I have said before of the waving-lines ; for as among the vast variety of waving-lines that may be conceived, there is but one that truly deserves the name of *the line of beauty*, so there is only one precise serpentine-line that I call *the line of grace*. Yet, even when they are made too bulging or too tapering, though they certainly lose of their beauty and grace, they do not become so wholly void of it, as not to be of excellent service in compositions, where beauty and grace are not particularly designed to be expressed in their greatest perfection.

Though I have distinguished these lines so particularly as to give them the titles of *the lines of beauty and grace*, I mean that the use and application of them should still be confined by the principles I P. have laid down for composition in general; and that they should be judiciously mixed and combined with one another, and even with those I may term *plain* lines, (in opposition to these), as the subject in hand requires. Thus the cornu-copia, fig. *, is twisted and bent after the same manner as the last figure of the horn, but more ornamented, and with a greater number of other lines of the same twisted kind, winding round it with as quick returns as those of a screw.

This sort of form may be seen with yet more variations (and therefore more beautiful) in the goat's horn, from which, in all probability, the ancients originally took the extreme elegant forms they have given their cornu-copias.

There is another way of considering this last figure of the horn I would recommend to my reader, in order to give him a clearer idea of the use both of the waving and serpentine-lines in composition.

This is to imagine the horn, thus bent and twisted, to be cut length-ways, by a very fine saw, into two equal parts; and to observe one of these in the same

* Fig. 59. B. p. 2.

position the whole horn is represented in, and these two observations will naturally occur to him : First, that the edge of the saw must run from one end to the other of the horn in the line of beauty, so that the edges of this half of the horn will have a beautiful shape ; and, secondly, that wherever the dotted serpentine-line on the surface of the whole horn dips behind, and is lost to the eye, it immediately comes into sight on the hollow surface of the divided horn.

P. 54

The use I shall make of these observations will appear very considerable in the application of them to the human form, which we are next to attempt.

It will be sufficient, therefore, at present only to observe, first, that the whole horn acquires a beauty by its being thus gently bent two different ways ; secondly, that whatever lines are drawn on its external surface become graceful, as they must all of them, from the twist that is given the horn, partake in some degree or other of the shape of the serpentine-line ; and, lastly, when the horn is split, and the inner as well as the outward surface of its shell-like form is exposed, the eye is peculiarly entertained and relieved in the pursuit of these serpentine-lines, as, in their twistings, their concavities and convexities are alternately offered to its view. Hollow forms, therefore, composed of such lines, are extremely beautiful and pleasing to the eye, in many cases more so than those of solid bodies.

Almost all the muscles and bones of which the human form is composed have more or less of these kind of twists in them, and give, in a less degree, the same kind of appearance to the parts which cover them, and are the immediate object of the eye; and for this reason it is that I have been so particular in describing these forms of the bent, and twisted, and ornamented horn.

There is scarce a straight bone in the whole body: **P. 55** almost all of them are not only bent different ways, but have a kind of twist, which in some of them is very graceful; and the muscles annexed to them, though they are of various shapes, appropriated to their particular uses, generally have their component fibres running in these serpentine-lines, surrounding and conforming themselves to the varied shapes of the bones they belong to; more especially in the limbs. Anatomists are so satisfied of this, that they take a pleasure in distinguishing their several beauties. I shall only instance in the thigh-bone, and those about the hips.

The thigh-bone, fig. *, has the waving and twisted turn of the horn, 58; but the beautiful bones adjoining, called the ossa innominata †, have, with greater variety, the same turns and twists of that horn when it is cut; and its inner and outward surfaces are exposed to the eye.

How ornamental these bones appear when the prejudice we conceive against them, as being part of a skeleton, is taken off, by adding a little foliage to them, may be seen in fig. ‡—Such shell-like winding forms, mixed with foliage twisting about them, are made use of in all ornaments; a kind of composition calculated merely to please the eye. Divest these of their serpentine twinings, and they imme-

---

* Fig. 62. R. p. 2.　† Fig. 60. B. p. 2.　‡ Fig. 61. B. p. 2.

djately lose all grace, and return to the poor Gothic taste they were in an hundred years ago.*

56   Fig. † is meant to represent the manner in which most of the muscles (those of the limbs in particular) are twisted round the bones, and conform themselves to their length and shape, but with no anatomical exactness. As to the running of their fibres, some anatomists have compared them to skains of thread, loose in the middle and tight at each end, which, when they are thus considered as twisted contrary ways round the bone, give the strongest idea possible of a composition of serpentine-lines.

Of these fine winding forms then are the muscles and bones of the human body composed, and which, by their varied situations with each other, become more intricately pleasing, and form a continued waving of winding forms from one into the other, as may be best seen by examining a good anatomical figure, part of which you have here represented, in the muscular leg and thigh, fig. ‡; which shows the serpentine forms and varied situations of the muscles, as they appear when the skin is taken off. It was drawn from a plaster of paris figure cast off nature, the original of which was prepared for the mould by Cowper, the famous anatomist. In this last figure, as the skin is taken off the parts are too distinctly traced by the eye, for that intricate delicacy which is necessary to the utmost beauty, yet the winding figures of the muscles, with the variety of their situations, must always be allowed elegant forms: however,

* Fig. 63. B. p. 2.   † Fig. 64. B. p. 2.   ‡ Fig. 65. p. 1.

they lose in the imagination some of the beauty which they really have, by the idea of their being flayed; nevertheless, by what has already been shewn P. both of them and the bones, the human frame hath more of its parts composed of serpentine-lines than any other object in nature, which is a proof both of its superior beauty to all others, and, at the same time, that its beauty proceeds from those lines: for although they may be required sometimes to be bulging in their twists, as in the thick swelling muscles of the Hercules, yet elegance and greatness of taste is still preserved; but when these lines lose so much of their twists as to become almost straight, all elegance of taste vanishes.

Thus fig. * was also taken from nature, and drawn in the same position, but treated in a more dry, stiff, and what the painters call, *sticky manner*, than the nature of flesh is ever capable of appearing in, unless when its moisture is dryed away: it must be allowed, that the parts of this figure are of as right dimensions, and as truly situated, as in the former; it wants only the true twist of the lines to give it taste.

To prove this further, and to put the mean effect of these plain or unvaried lines in a stronger light, see fig. †, where, by the uniform, unvaried shapes and situation of the muscles, without so much as a waving-line in them, it becomes so wooden a form, that he that can fashion the leg of a joint-stool may carve this figure as well as the best sculptor. In the same manner, divest one of the best antique statues of all

* Fig. 66. P. 1.   † Fig. 67. P. 1.

P. 58 its serpentine winding parts, and it becomes from an exquisite piece of art, a figure of such ordinary lines and unvaried contents, that a common stone-mason or carpenter, with the help of his rule, calipers, and compasses, might carve out an exact imitation of it: and were it not for these lines, a turner, in his lathe, might turn a much finer neck than that of the Grecian Venus, as, according to the common notion of a beautiful neck, it would be more truly round. For the same reason, legs much swollen with disease are as easy to imitate as a post, having lost their *drawing*, as the painters call it; that is, having their serpentine-lines all effaced by the skin's being equally puffed up, as figure *.

If, in comparing these three figures one with another, the reader, notwithstanding the prejudice his imagination may have conceived against them, as anatomical figures, has been enabled only to perceive that one of them is not so disagreeable as the others, he will easily be led to see further, that this tendency to beauty in one is not owing to any greater degree of exactness in the *proportions* of its parts, but merely to the more *pleasing turns and intertwistings of the lines* which compose its external form; for in all the three figures the same proportions have been observed, and, on that account, they have all an equal claim to beauty.

And if he pursues this anatomical enquiry but a very little further, just to form a true idea of the elegant use that is made of the skin and fat beneath it, P. 59 to conceal from the eye all that is hard and disagree-

---

* Fig. 68.

able, and at the same time to preserve to it whatever is necessary in the shapes of the parts beneath, to give grace and beauty to the whole limb: he will find himself insensibly led into the principles of that grace and beauty which is to be found in well-turned limbs in fine, elegant, healthy life, or in those of the best antique statues; as well as into the reason why his eye has so often unknowingly been pleased and delighted with them.

Thus, in all other parts of the body as well as these, wherever, for the sake of the necessary motion of the parts, with proper strength and agility, the insertions of the muscles are too hard and sudden, their swellings too bold, or the hollows between them too deep for their out-lines to be beautiful, nature most judiciously softens these hardnesses, and plumps up these vacancies with a proper supply of fat, and covers the whole with the soft, smooth, springy, and, in delicate life, almost transparent skin, which, conforming itself to the external shape of all the parts beneath, expresses to the eye the idea of its contents with the utmost delicacy of beauty and grace.

The skin, therefore, thus tenderly embracing and gently conforming itself to the varied shapes of every one of the outward muscles of the body, softened underneath by the fat, where, otherwise, the same hard lines and furrows would appear, as we find come on with age in the face, and with labour in the limbs, is evidently a shell-like surface, (to keep up the idea I P. set out with,) formed with the utmost delicacy in nature; and therefore the most proper subject of the study of every one who desires to imitate the works.

E

of nature. *as a master should do*, or to judge of the performances of others *as a real connoisseur ought*.

I cannot be too long, I think, on this subject, as so much will be found to depend upon it : and therefore shall endeavour to give a clear idea of the different effect such anatomical figures have on the eye, from what the same parts have when covered by the fat and skin, by supposing a small wire (that has lost its spring. and so will retain every shape it is twisted into) to be held fast to the outside of the hip, (fig. 65, plate I.) and thence brought down the other side of the thigh obliquely over the calf of the leg, down to the outward ancle, (all the while pressed so close as to touch and conform itself to the shape of every muscle it passes over.) and then to be taken off. If this wire be now examined. it will be found that the general uninterrupted flowing twist, which the winding round the limbs would otherwise have given to it, is broke into little better than so many separate plain curves, by the sharp indentures it every where has received on being closely pressed in between the muscles.

Suppose, in the next place, such a wire was in the same manner twisted round a living well-shaped leg and thigh, or those of a fine statue, when you take it off you will find no such sharp indentures, nor any of those regular *engralings* (as the heralds express it) which displeased the eye before. On the contrary, you will see how *gradually* the changes in its shape are produced, how imperceptibly the different curvatures run into each other, and how easily the eye glides along the varied wavings of its sweep. To enforce this still further, if a line was to be drawn by a

P. 61

pencil exactly where these wires have been supposed to pass, the point of the pencil, in the muscular leg and thigh, would perpetually meet with stops and rubs, whilst in the others it would flow from muscle to muscle along the elastic skin, as pleasantly as the lightest skiff dances over the gentlest wave.

This idea of the wire, retaining thus the shape of the parts it passes over, seems of so much consequence, that I would by no means have it forgot, as it may properly be considered as one of the threads (or outlines) of the shell (or external surface) of the human form : and the frequently recurring to it will assist the imagination in its conceptions of those parts of it whose shapes are most intricately varied : for the same sort of observations may be made with equal justice on the shapes of ever so many such wires, twisted in the same manner in ever so many directions over every part of a well-made man, woman, or statue.

And if the reader will follow in his imagination the most exquisite turns of the chissel in the hands of a master, when he is putting the finishing touches to a statue, he will soon be led to understand what it is the real judges expect from the hand of such a master, which the Italians call, the little more, *Il poco piu*, and which in reality distinguishes the original master-pieces at Rome from even the best copies of them.

An example or two will sufficiently explain what is here meant ; for as these exquisite turns are to be found in some degree of beauty or other, all over the whole surface of the body and limbs, we may, by taking any one part of a fine figure (though so small

P.62

a one that only a few muscles are expressed in it,) explain the manner in which so much beauty and grace has been given to them, as to convince a skilful artist, almost at sight, that it must have been the work of a master.

I have chosen, for this purpose, a small piece of the body of a statue, fig. *, representing part of the left side under the arm, together with a little of the breast, (including a very particular muscle, which, from the likeness its edges bear to the teeth of a saw, is, if considered by itself, void of beauty,) as most proper to the point in hand, because this its regular shape more peculiarly requires the skill of the artist to give it a little more variety than it generally has, even in nature.

First, then, I will give you a representation of this part of the body, from an anatomical figure †, to show what a sameness there is in the shapes of all the teeth-like insertions of this muscle; and how regularly the fibres, which compose it, follow the almost parallel outlines of the ribs they partly cover.

P. 63 From what has been said before of the use of the natural covering of the skin, &c. the next figure ‡ will easily be understood to mean so tame a representation of the same part of the body, that though the hard and stiff appearance of the edges of this muscle is taken off by that covering, yet enough of its regularity and sameness remains to render it disagreeable.

Now as regularity and sameness, according to our doctrine, is want of elegance and true taste, we shall

* Fig. 76. T. p. 2.   † Fig. 77. T. p. 2.   ‡ Fig. 78. T. p. 2.

endeavour in the next place to shew how this very part (in which the muscles take so very regular a form) may be brought to have as much variety as any other part of the body whatever. In order to this, though some alteration must be made in almost every part of it, yet it should be so inconsiderable in each, that no remarkable change may appear in the shape and situation of any.

Thus, let the parts marked 1, 2, 3, 4, (which appear so exactly similar in shape, and parallel in situation in the muscular figure 77,) and not much mended in fig. 78, be first varied in their sizes, but not gradually from the uppermost to the lowest, as in fig.*, nor alternately one long and one short, as in fig.†, for in either of these cases there would still remain too great a formality. We should therefore endeavour, in the next place, to vary them every way in our power, without losing entirely the true idea of the parts themselves. Suppose them then to have changed their situations a little, and slipped beside each other P. irregularly, (some how as is represented in fig. ‡, merely with regard to situation,) and the external appearance of the whole piece of the body, now under our consideration, will assume the more varied and pleasing form represented in fig. 76, easily to be discerned by comparing the three figures 76, 77, 78, one with another, and it will as easily be seen, that were lines to be drawn, or wires to be bent, over these muscles, from one to the other, and so on to the adjoining

* Fig. 79. T. p. 2. † Fig. 80. T. p. 2. ‡ Fig. 81. T. p. 2.

parts, they would have a continued waving flow, let them pass in any direction whatever.

The unskilful, in drawing these parts after the life, as their regularities are much more easily seen and copied than their fine variations, seldom fail of making them more regular and poor than they really appear even in a consumptive person.

The difference will appear evident by comparing fig. 78, purposely drawn in this tasteless manner, with fig. 76. But will be more perfectly understood by examining this part in the Torso of Michael Angelo,* whence this figure was taken.

Note—There are casts of a small copy of that famous trunk of a body to be had at almost every plaster-figure maker's, wherein what has been here described may be sufficiently seen, not only in the part which figure 76 was taken from, but all over that curious piece of antiquity.

P. 65   I must here again press my reader to a particular attention to the windings of these superficial lines, even in their passing over every joint, what alterations soever may be made in the surface of the skin by the various bendings of the limbs : and though the space allowed for it, just in the joints, be ever so small, and consequently the lines ever so short, the application of this principle of varying these lines, as far as their lengths will admit of, will be found to have its effect as gracefully as in the more lengthened muscles of the body.

* Fig. 54. p. 1.

It should be observed in the fingers, where the joints are but short, and the tendons straight; and where beauty seems to submit, in some degree, to use, yet not so much but you trace, in a full-grown taper finger, these little winding lines among the wrinkles, or in (what is more pretty because more simple) the dimples of the nuckles. As we always distinguish things best by seeing their reverse set in opposition with them, if fig. *, by the straightness of its lines, shews fig. †, to have some little taste in it, though it is so slightly sketched, the difference will more evidently appear when you in like manner compare a straight coarse finger in common life with the taper dimpled one of a fine lady.

There is an elegant degree of plumpness peculiar to the skin of the softer sex, that occasions these delicate dimplings in all their other joints as well as these of the fingers, which so perfectly distinguishes them from those even of a graceful man, and which, assisted by the more softened shapes of the muscles underneath, presents to the eye all the varieties in the whole figure of the body with gentler and fewer parts more sweetly connected together, and with such a fine simplicity as will always give the turn of the female frame, represented in the Venus ‡, the preference to that of the Apollo.§

Now whoever can conceive lines thus constantly flowing, and delicately varying over every part of the body, even to the fingers' ends, and will call to his

P. 66

* Fig. 82. T. p. 2.   † Fig. 83. T. p. 2.   ‡ Fig. 13. p. 1.
    § Fig. 12. p. 1.

remembrance what led us to this last description of what the Italians call, Il poco piu, (*the little more* that is expected from the hand of a master,) will, in my mind, want very little more than what his own observation on the works of art and nature will lead him to, to acquire a true idea of the word *taste*, when applied to form, however inexplicable this word may hitherto have been imagined.

We have all along had recourse chiefly to the works of the ancients, not because the moderns have not produced some as excellent; but because the works of the former are more generally known : nor would we have it thought, that either of them have ever yet come up to the utmost beauty of nature. Who but a bigot, even to the antiques, will say that he has not seen faces and necks, hands and arms, in living women, that even the Grecian Venus doth but coarsely imitate ?

P.67   And what sufficient reason can be given why the same may not be said of the rest of the body ?

CHAPTER XI.

OF PROPORTION.

IF any one should ask, what it is that constitutes a fine-proportioned human figure? how ready and seemingly decisive is the common answer, *a just symmetry and harmony of parts with respect to the whole*. But as probably this vague answer took its rise from doctrines not belonging to form, or idle schemes built on them, I apprehend it will cease to be thought much to the purpose after a proper enquiry has been made.

Preparatory to which, it becomes necessary in this place to mention one reason more which may be added to those given in the introduction, for my having persuaded the reader to consider objects scooped out like thin shells, which is, that partly by this conception he may be the better able to separate and keep asunder the two following *general ideas*, as we will call them, belonging to form, which are apt to coincide and mix with each other in the mind, and which it is necessary (for the sake of making each more fully and particularly clear,) should be kept apart and considered singly.

First, the *general ideas* of what hath already been discussed in the foregoing chapters, which only comprehends the surface of form, viewing it in no other light than merely as being ornamental or not.

P. 68 Secondly, that *general idea*, now to be discussed, which we commonly have of form altogether, as arising chiefly from a fitness to some designed purpose or use.

Hitherto our main drift hath been to establish and illustrate the first idea only, by showing first the nature of variety, and then its effects on the mind ; with the manner how such impressions are made by means of the different feelings given to the eye, from its movements in tracing and coursing* over surfaces of all kinds.

The surface of a piece of ornament, that hath every turn in it that lines are capable of moving into, and at the same time no way applied, nor of any manner of use but merely to entertain the eye, would be such an object as would answer to this first idea alone.

The figure like a leaf, at the bottom of plate 1, near to fig. 67, is something of this kind ; it was taken from an ash-tree, and was a sort of *lusus naturæ*, growing only like an excrescence, but so beautiful in the lines of its shell-like windings as would have been above the power of a Gibbons to have equalled, even in its own materials ; nor could the graver of an Edlinck or Drevet have done it justice on copper.

Note—The present taste of ornaments seems to have been partly taken from productions of this sort,

* See Chap. V. p. 25.

which are to be found about autumn among plants, particularly asparagus, when it is running to seed.

P. 69

I shall now endeavour to explain what is included in what I have called, for distinction sake, the second *general idea* of form, in a much fuller manner than was done in chapter I. of Fitness; and begin with observing, that though surfaces will unavoidably be still included, yet we must no longer confine ourselves to the particular notice of them as surfaces only, as we heretofore have done; we must now open our view to general as well as particular bulk and solidity; and also look into what may have filled up or given rise thereto, such as certain *given* quantities and dimensions of parts, for inclosing any substance, or for performing of *motion, purchase, stedfastness*, and other matters of use to living beings, which, I apprehend, at length, will bring us to a tolerable conception of the word *proportion*.

As to these *joint-sensations* of bulk and motion, do we not, at first sight almost, even without making trial, seem to *feel* when a lever of any kind is too weak, or not long enough, to make such or such a purchase? or when a spring is not sufficient? and don't we find by experience what weight or dimension should be given or taken away on this or that account? if so, as the general as well as particular bulks of form are made up of materials moulded together under mechanical directions, for some known purpose or other, how naturally, from these considerations, shall we fall into a judgment of *fit proportion;* which is one part of beauty to the mind, though not always so to the eye.

P. 70 Our necessities have taught us to mould matter into various shapes, and to give them fit proportions for particular uses, as bottles, glasses, knives, dishes, &c. Hath not offence given rise to the form of the sword, and defence to that of the shield? And what else but proper fitness of parts hath fixed the different dimensions of pistols, common guns, great guns, fowling-pieces, and blunderbusses; which differences, as to figure, may as properly be called the different characters of fire-arms, as the different shapes of men are called characters of men.

We find also that the profuse variety of shapes which present themselves from the whole animal creation, arise chiefly from the nice fitness of their parts, designed for accomplishing the peculiar movements of each.

And here I think will be the proper place to speak of a most curious difference between the living machines of nature, in respect of fitness, and such poor ones, in comparison with them, as men are only capable of making; by means of which distinction, I am in hopes of showing what particularly constitutes the utmost beauty of proportion in the human figure.

A clock, by the government's order, has been made, and another now making, by Mr Harrison, for the keeping of true time at sea, which perhaps is one of the most exquisite movements ever made. Happy the ingenious contriver! although the form of the whole, or of every part of this curious machine, P. 71 should be ever so confused, or displeasingly shaped to the eye, and although even its movements should be disagreeable to look at, provided it answers the

I

end proposed: an ornamental composition was no part of his scheme, otherwise than as a polish might be necessary; if ornaments are required to be added to mend its shape, care must be taken that they are no obstruction to the movement itself, and the more as they would be superfluous as to the main design. —But in Nature's machines, how wonderfully do we see beauty and use go hand in hand!

Had a machine for this purpose been Nature's work, the whole and every individual part might have had exquisite beauty of form without danger of destroying the exquisiteness of its motion, even as if ornament had been the sole aim; its movements too might have been graceful, without one superfluous tittle added for either of these lovely purposes.—Now this is that curious difference between the fitness of Nature's machines (one of which is man) and those made by mortal hands; which distinction is to lead us to our main point proposed, I mean to the showing what constitutes the utmost beauty of proportion.

There was brought from France some years ago, a little clock-work machine, with a duck's head and legs fixt to it, which was so contrived as to have some resemblance to that animal standing upon one foot, and stretching back its leg, turning its head, opening and shutting its bill, moving its wings, and shaking its tail; all of them the plainest and easiest direc- P. tions in living movements; yet for the poorly performing of these few motions, this silly, but much extolled machine, being uncovered, appeared a most complicated, confused, and disagreeable object: nor would its being covered with a skin closely adhering to its parts as that of a real duck's doth, have much mended its figure; at best a bag of hob-nails, broken hinges, and patten-rings, would have looked as well, unless by other means it had been stuffed out to bring it into form.

Thus, again, you see the more variety we pretend to give to our trifling movements, the more confused and unornamental the forms become, nay, chance but seldom helps them——How much the reverse are Nature's! the greater the variety her movements have, the more beautiful are the parts that cause them.

The finny race of animals, as they have fewer motions than other creatures, so are their forms less remarkable for beauty. It is also to be noted of every species that the handsomest of each move best: birds of a clumsy make seldom fly well, nor do lumpy fish glide so well through the water as those of a neater make; and beasts of the most elegant form always excel in speed; of this the horse and greyhound are beautiful examples; and even among themselves the most elegantly made seldom fail of being the swiftest.

P. 73 The war-horse is more equally made for strength than the race-horse, which surplus of power in the former, if supposed added to the latter, as it would throw more weight into improper parts for the business of mere speed, so of course it would lessen in some degree that admirable quality, and partly destroy that delicate fitness of his make; but then a quality in movement, superior to that of speed, would be given to him by the addition, as he would be rendered thereby more fit to move with ease in such varied or graceful directions as are so delightful to the eye in the carriage of the fine managed war-horse, and at the same time something stately and graceful would be added to his figure. which before could only be said to have an elegant neatness. This noble creature stands foremost amongst brutes ; and it is but consistent with Nature's propriety, that the most useful animal in the brute creation should be thus signalized also for the most beauty.

Yet, properly speaking, no living creatures are capable of moving in such truly varied and graceful directions as the human species ; and it would be needless to say how much superior in beauty their forms and textures likewise are. And surely also, after what has been said relating to figure and motion, it is plain and evident that Nature has thought fit to make beauty of proportion and beauty of movement necessary to each other ; so that the observation before made on animals will hold equally good with regard to man ; *i. e.* that he who is most exquisitely well proportioned is most capable of exquisite movements, such as ease and *grace in deportment*, or in dancing.

It may be a sort of collateral confirmation of what P. 74 has been said of this method of Nature's working, as well as otherwise worth our notice, that when any parts belonging to the human body are concealed, and not immediately concerned in movement, all such ornamental shapes, as evidently appear in the muscles and bones,* are totally neglected as unnecessary, for Nature doth nothing in vain : this is plainly

* See Chap. IX. on Compositions with the Serpentine-Line.

the case of the intestines, none of them having the least beauty as to form except the *heart;* which noble part, and indeed kind of first mover, is a simple and well-varied figure, conformable to which some of the most elegant Roman urns and vases have been fashioned.

Now, thus much being kept in remembrance, our next step will be to speak of, first, general measurements, such as the whole height of the body to its breadth, or the length of a limb to its thickness; and, secondly, of such appearances of dimensions as are too intricately varied to admit of a description by lines.

The former will be confined to a very few straight lines, crossing each other, which will easily be understood by every one; but the latter will require somewhat more attention, because it will extend to the precision of every modification, bound, or limit of the human figure.

To be somewhat more explicit. As to the first part, I shall begin with showing what practicable sort of measuring may be used in order to produce the most proper variety in the proportions of the parts of any body. I say *practicable,* because the vast variety of intricately situated parts belonging to the human form, will not admit of measuring the distances of one part by another, by lines or points, beyond a certain degree or number, without great perplexity in the operation itself, or confusion to the imagination. For instance say, a line representing one breadth and an half of the wrist, would be equal to the true breadth of the thickest part of the arm above the elbow, may it not then be asked, what part of the

P. 75

wrist is meant? for if you place a pair of calipers a
little nearer or further from the hand, the distance
of the points will differ, and so they will if they are
moved close to the wrist all round, because it is flat-
ter one way than the other; but suppose, for argument sake, one certain diameter should be fixed
upon, may it not again be asked, how it is to be applied, if to the flattest side of the arm or the roundest,
and how far from the elbow, and must it be when
the arm is extended or when it is bent? for this also
will make a sensible difference, because in the latter
position the muscle, called the biceps, in the front
of that part of the arm, swells up like a ball one way,
and narrows itself another; nay, all the muscles shift
their appearances in different movements, so that
whatever may have been pretended by some authors,
no exact mathematical measurements by lines can
be given for the true proportion of a human body.

It comes then to this, that no longer than whilst P. 76
we suppose all the lengths and breadths of the body,
or limbs, to be as regular figures as cylinders, or as
the leg, figure 68 in plate 1, which is as round as a
rolling stone, are the measures of lengths to breadths
practicable, or of any use to the knowledge of proportion: so that as all mathematical schemes are foreign
to this purpose, we will endeavour to root them quite
out of our way: therefore I must not omit taking
notice, that Albert Durer, Lamozzo, (see two tasteless figures taken from their books of proportion,*)
and some others, have not only puzzled mankind

* Fig. 55. p. 1.

with a heap of minute unnecessary divisions, but also with a strange *notion* that those divisions are governed by the laws of music, which mistake they seem to have been led into by having seen certain uniform and consonant divisions upon one string produce harmony to the ear, and by persuading themselves that similar distances in lines belonging to form would, in like manner, delight the eye. The very reverse of which has been shewn to be true, in Chap. 3, on Uniformity. "The length of the foot, say they, in respect to the breadth, makes a *double suprabipartient*, a *diapason* and a *diatesseron:*"[*] which, P. 77 in my opinion, would have been full as applicable to the ear, or to a plant, or to a tree, or any other form whatsoever; yet these sort of *notions* have so far prevailed by time, that the words, *harmony of parts*, seem as applicable to form as to music.

Notwithstanding the absurdity of the above schemes, such measures as are to be taken from antique statues may be of some service to painters and sculptors, especially to young beginners, but nothing nigh of such use to them as the measures, taken the same way from ancient buildings, have been, and are, to architects and builders; because the latter have to do with little else but plain geometrical fi-

---

[*] Note—These authors assure you, that this curious method of measuring *will produce beauty far beyond any nature doth afford.* Lamozzo recommends also another scheme, with a triangle, to correct the *poverty of nature*, as they express themselves. These *naturemenders* put one in mind of Gulliver's tailor at Laputa, who, having taken measure of him for a suit of clothes with a rule, quadrant, and compasses, after a considerable time spent, brought them home ill made.

gures : which measures, however, serve only in copying what has been done before.

The few measures I shall speak of, for the setting
out the general dimensions of a figure, shall be taken
by straight lines only, for the more easy conception
of what may indeed be properly called, *gaging the
contents of the body*, supposing it solid like a marble
statue, as the wires were described to do * in the introduction : by which plain method clear ideas may
be acquired of what *alone* seem to me to require
measuring, of what certain lengths to what breadths
make the most eligible proportions in general.

The most general dimensions of a body, or limbs,
are lengths, breadths, or thicknesses : now the whole
gentility of a figure, according to its character, depends upon the first proportioning these lines, or
wires, (which are its measures,) properly one to another ; and the more varied these lines are with respect to each other, the more may the future divisions be varied likewise that are to be made on them ;
and of course the less varied these lines are, the parts
influenced by them, as they must conform themselves
to them, must have less variety too. For example,
the exact cross † of two equal lines, cutting each
other in the middle, would confine the figure of a
man, drawn conformable to them, to the disagreeable
character of his being as broad as he is long. And the
two lines crossing each other, to make the height
and breadth of a figure, will want variety a contrary
way, by one line being very short in proportion to the

P. 78

* Fig. 2. p. 1.   † Fig. 69. R. p. 2.

other, and therefore also incapable of producing a figure of tolerable variety. To prove this, it will be very easy for the reader to make the experiment, by drawing a figure or two (though ever so imperfectly) confined within such limits.

There is a medium between these, proper for every character, which the eye will easily and accurately determine.

Thus, if the lines, fig. *, were to be the measure of the extreme length and breadth, set out either for the figure of a man or a vase, the eye soon sees the longest of these is not quite sufficiently so, in proportion to the other, for a genteel man, and yet it would make
P. 79   a vase too taper to be elegant; no rule or compasses would decide this matter either so quickly or so precisely as a good eye. It may be observed, that minute differences in great lengths are of little or no consequence as to proportion, because they are not to be discerned; for a man is half an inch shorter when he goes to bed at night, than when he rises in the morning, without the possibility of its being perceived. In case of a wager, the application of a rule or compasses may be necessary, but seldom on any other occasion.

Thus much I apprehend is sufficient for the consideration of general lengths to breadths. Where, by the way, I apprehend I have plainly shewn, that there is no practicable rule, by lines, for minutely setting out proportions *for* the human body, and if there were, the eye alone must determine us in our choice of what is most pleasing to itself.

* Fig. 70. R. p. 2.

Thus having dispatched general dimension, which we may say is almost as much of proportion as is to be seen when we have our clothes on, I shall in the second, and more extensive method proposed for considering it, set out in the familiar path of common observation, and appeal, as I go on, to our usual feeling, or joint-sensation, of figure and motion.

Perhaps by mentioning two or three known instances, it will be found that almost every one is farther advanced in the knowledge of this speculative part of proportion than he imagines ; especially he who hath been used to observe naked figures doing P. 80 bodily exercise, and more especially if he be any way interested in the success of them ; and the better he is acquainted with the nature of the exercise itself, still the better judge he becomes of the figure that is to perform it. For this reason, no sooner are two boxers stript to fight, but even a butcher, thus skilled, shews himself a considerable critic in proportion ; and on this sort of judgment often gives or takes the odds, at bare sight only of the combatants. I have heard a blacksmith harangue like an anatomist, or sculptor, on the beauty of a boxer's figure, though not perhaps in the same terms ; and I firmly believe, that one of our common proficients in the athletic art would be able to instruct and direct the best sculptor living (who hath not seen, or is wholly ignorant of this exercise) in what would give the statue of an English boxer a much better proportion, as to character, than is to be seen even in the famous group of antique boxers (or, as some call them, Roman wrestlers) so much admired to this day.

I

Indeed, as many parts of the body are so constantly kept covered, the proportion of the whole cannot be equally known; but as stockings are so close and thin a covering, every one judges of the different shapes and proportions of legs with great accuracy. The ladies always speak skilfully of necks, hands, and arms; and often will point out such particular beauties or defects in their make, as might easily escape the observation of a man of science.

81   Surely such determinations could not be made and pronounced with such critical truth, if the eye were not capable of measuring or judging of thicknesses by lengths with great preciseness. Nay, more, in order to determine so nicely as they often do, it must also at the same time trace with some skill those delicate windings upon the surface which have been described in page 64 and 65, which altogether may be observed to include the two general ideas mentioned at the beginning of this chapter.

If so, certainly it is in the power of a man of science, with as observing an eye, to go still further, and conceive, with a very little turn of thought, many other necessary circumstances concerning proportion, as of what size and in what manner the bones help to make up the bulk, and support the other parts; as well as what certain weights or dimensions of muscles are proper (according to the principle of the steel-yard) to move such or such a length of arm with this or that degree of swiftness or force.

But though much of this matter may be easily understood by common observation, assisted by science, still I fear it will be difficult to raise a very clear idea of what constitutes or composes the *utmost beauty of proportion*; such as is seen in the Antinous, which is allowed to be the most perfect, in this respect, of any of the antique statues; and though the lovely likewise seems to have been as much the sculptor's aim, as in the Venus, yet a manly strength in its pro- P. 82 portion is equally expressed from head to foot in it.

Let us try, however, and as this master-piece of art is so well known, we will set it up before us as a pattern, and endeavour to fabricate, or put together in the mind, such kind of parts as shall seem to build another figure like it. In doing which we shall soon find that it is chiefly to be effected by means of the nice sensation we naturally have of what certain quantities, or dimensions of parts, are fittest to produce the utmost strength for moving or supporting great weights; and of what are most fit for the utmost light agility, as also for every degree between these two extremes.

He who hath best perfected his ideas of these matters by common observations, and by the assistance of arts relative thereto, will probably be most precisely just and clear in conceiving the application of the various parts and dimensions that will occur to him in the following descriptive manner of disposing of them, in order to form the idea of a fine-proportioned figure.

Having set up the Antinous as our pattern, we will suppose there were placed on one side of it the unwieldy elephant-like figure of an Atlas, made up of such thick bones and muscles as would best fit him for supporting a vast weight, according to his character of extreme heavy strength: and, on the other side, P. 83

imagine the slim figure of a Mercury, every where neatly formed for the utmost light agility, with slender bones and taper muscles fit for his nimble bounding from the ground.—Both these figures must be supposed of equal height, and not exceeding six foot.[1]

Our *extremes* thus placed, now imagine the Atlas throwing off by degrees certain portions of bone and muscle, proper for the attainment of light agility, as if aiming at the Mercury's airy form and quality, whilst on the other hand, see the Mercury augmenting his taper figure by equal degrees, and growing towards an Atlas in equal time, by receiving to the like places from whence they came, the very quantities that the other had been casting off, when, as they approach each other in weight, their forms of course may be imagined to grow more and more alike, till, at a certain point of time, they meet in just similitude, which being an exact medium between the two extremes, we may thence conclude it to be the precise form of exact proportion fittest for perfect active strength or graceful movement, such as the Antinous we proposed to imitate and figure in the mind.[2]

I am apprehensive that this part of my scheme, for

[1] If the scale of either of these proportions were to exceed six foot in the life, the quality of strength in one, and agility in the other, would gradually decrease the larger the person grew. There are sufficient proofs of this, both from mechanical reasonings and common observation.

[2] The jockey, who knows to an ounce what flesh or bone in a horse is fittest for speed or strength, will as easily conceive the like process between the strongest dray-horse and the fleetest racer, and soon conclude, that the fine war-horse must be the medium between the two extremes.

explaining exact proportion, may not be thought so
sufficiently determinate as could be wished ; be this P. 84
as it will, I must submit it to the reader as my best
resource in so difficult a case, and shall therefore beg
leave to try to illustrate it a little more, by observing,
that, in like manner, any two opposite colours in the
rainbow form a third between them, by thus impart-
ing to each other their peculiar qualities ; as, for
example, the brightest yellow, and the lively blue
that is placed at some distance from it, visibly approach, and blend by interchangeable degrees, and,
as above, *temper* rather than destroy each other's vi-
gour, till they meet in one firm compound, whence,
at a certain point, the sight of what they were originally is quite lost ; but in their stead a most pleasing green is found, which colour Nature hath chose
for the vestment of the earth, and with the beauty
of which the eye is never tired.

From the order of the ideas which the description
of the above three figures may have raised in the mind,
we may easily compose between them various other
proportions. And as the painter, by means of a certain order in the arrangement of the colours upon his
pallet, readily mixes up what kind of tint he pleases,
so may we mix up and compound in the imagination
such fit parts as will be consistent with this or that
particular character, or at least be able thereby to
discover how such characters are composed when
we see them either in art or nature.

But perhaps even the word *character, as it relates to* P. 85
form, may not be quite understood by every one,
though it is so frequently used, nor do I remember to

have seen it explained any where. Therefore on this account, and also as it will further show the use of thinking of form and motion together, it will not be improper to observe, that, notwithstanding a character in this sense chiefly depends on a figure being remarkable as to its form, either in some particular part or altogether, yet surely no figure, be it ever so singular, can be perfectly conceived as a character, till we find it connected with some remarkable circumstance or cause, for such particularity of appearance; for instance, a fat bloated person doth not call to mind the character of a Silenus, till we have joined the idea of voluptuousness with it; so likewise strength to support, and clumsiness of figure, are united as well in the character of an Atlas as in a porter.

When we consider the great weight chairmen often have to carry, do we not readily consent that there is a propriety and fitness in the Tuscan order of their legs, by which they properly become *characters* as to figure?

Watermen, too, are of a distinct cast or character, whose legs are no less remarkable for their smallness; for, as there is naturally the greatest call for nutriment to the parts that are most exercised, so of course these that lie so much stretched out are apt to dwindle, or not grow to their full size. P. 86 There is scarcely a waterman that rows upon the Thames whose figure doth not confirm this observation. Therefore, were I to paint the character of a Charon, I would thus distinguish his make from that of a common man's, and, in spite of the word *low,* venture to give him a broad pair of shoulders and spindle shanks, whether I had the authority of an antique statue, or basso-relievo, for it or not.

May be I cannot throw a stronger light on what has been hitherto said of proportion, than by animadverting on a remarkable beauty in the Apollo-Belvedere, which hath given it the preference even to the Antinous: I mean a super addition of *greatness*, to at least as much beauty and grace as is found in the latter.

These two master-pieces of art are seen together in the same palace at Rome, where the Antinous fills the spectator with admiration only, whilst the Apollo strikes him with surprise, and, as travellers express themselves, with an appearance of something *more than human;* which they of *course* are always at a loss to describe; and this effect, they say, is the more astonishing, as, upon examination, its disproportion is evident even to a common eye. One of the best sculptors we have in England, who lately went to see them, confirmed to me what has been now said, particularly as to the legs and thighs being too long and too large for the upper parts. And Andrea Sacchi, one of the great Italian painters, seems to have been of the same opinion, or he would hardly have given his Apollo, crowning Pasquilini P. the musician, the exact proportion of the Antinous (in a famous picture of his now in England,) as otherwise it seems to be a direct copy from the Apollo.

Although in very great works we often see an inferior part neglected, yet here it cannot be the case, because in a fine statue just proportion is one of its essential beauties ; therefore it stands to reason that these limbs must have been lengthened on purpose, otherwise it might easily have been avoided.

So that if we examine the beauties of this figure thoroughly, we may reasonably conclude that what has been hitherto thought so unaccountably *excellent* in its general appearance, hath been owing to what hath seemed a *blemish* in a part of it ; but let us endeavour to make this matter as clear as possible, as it may add more force to what has been said.

Statues by being bigger than life (as this is one, and larger than the Antinous) always gain some nobleness in effect, according to the principle of quantity ; * but this alone is not sufficient to give what is properly to be called *greatness* in proportion ; for were figures 17 and 18, in plate 1, to be drawn or carved by a scale of ten feet high, they would still be but pigmy proportions, as, on the other hand, a figure of but two inches may represent a gigantic height.

Therefore *greatness* of proportion must be considered as depending on the application of *quantity* to those parts of the body where it can give more scope to its grace in movement, as to the neck for the larger and swan-like turns of the head, and to the legs and thighs for the more ample sway of all the upper parts together.

By which we find that the Antinous's being equally magnified to the Apollo's height, would not sufficiently produce that superiority of effect as to greatness so evidently seen in the latter.   The additions

* See Chap. VI.

necessary to the production of this *greatness* in proportion as it there appears added to grace, must then be by the proper application of them to the parts mentioned only.

I know not how further to prove this matter than by appealing to the reader's eye and common observation as before.

The Antinous being allowed to have the justest proportion possible, let us see what addition, upon the principle of quantity, can be made to it without taking away any of its beauty.

If we imagine an addition of dimensions to the head, we shall immediately conceive it would only deform—if to the hands or feet, we are sensible of something gross and ungenteel—if to the whole length of the arms, we feel they would be dangling and awkward—if by an addition of length or breadth to the body, we know it would appear heavy and clumsy,—there remains then only the *neck*, with the *legs* and *thighs*, to speak of; but to these we find, that not only certain additions may be admitted without causing any disagreeable effect, but that thereby *greatness*, the last perfection as to proportion, is given to the human form, as is evidently P. 89 expressed in the Apollo; and may still be further confirmed by examining the drawings of Parmigiano, where these particulars are seen in excess; yet on this account his works are said, by all true connoisseurs, to have an inexpressible greatness of taste in them, though otherwise very incorrect.

Let us now return to the two general ideas we set out with at the beginning of this chapter, and recollect, that under the first, on surface, I have shewn in what manner and how far human proportion is measurable, by varying the contents of the body, conformable to the given proportion of two lines ; and that under the second and more extensive general idea of form, as arising from fitness for movement, &c. I have endeavoured to explain, by every means I could devise, that every particular and minute dimension of the body should conform to such purposes of movement, &c. as have been first properly considered and determined ; on which, conjunctively, the true proportion of every character must depend, and is found so to do, by our joint-sensation of bulk and motion. Which account of the proportion of the human body, however imperfect, may possibly stand its ground till one more plausible shall be given.

As the Apollo * has been only mentioned on account of the greatness of its proportion, I think, in justice to so fine a performance, and also as it is not foreign to the point we have been upon, we may subjoin an observation or two on its perfections.

Besides what is commonly allowed, if we consider it by the rules here given for constituting or composing character, it will discover the author's great sagacity in choosing a proportion for this deity which has served two noble purposes at once, in that these very dimensions which appear to have given it so much dignity, are the same that are best fitted to produce the utmost speed. And what could characterise the god of day, either so strongly or elegantly, to be expressive in a statue, as superior swift-

* Fig. 12. p. 1.

ness, and beauty dignified? and how poetically doth the action it is put into carry on the allusion to speed,* as he is lightly stepping forward, and seeming to shoot his arrows from him, if the arrows may be allowed to signify the sun's rays? This at least may as well be supposed as the common surmise that he is killing the dragon Python; which certainly is very inconsistent with so erect an attitude and benign an aspect.†

Nor are the inferior parts neglected; the drapery also that depends from his shoulders, and folds over his extended arm, hath its treble office; as, first, it assists in keeping the general appearance within the boundary of a pyramid, which being inverted, is for a single figure rather more natural and genteel than one upon its basis. Secondly, it fills up the vacant angle under the arm, and takes off the straightness of the lines the arms necessarily make with the body in such an action; and, lastly, spreading as it doth in pleasing folds, it helps to satisfy the eye with a noble quantity in the composition altogether, without depriving the beholder of any part of the beauties of the naked: in short, this figure might serve, were a lecture to be read over it, to exemplify every principle that hath been hitherto advanced. We shall therefore close not only all we have to say on proportion with it, but our whole lineal account of form, except what we have particularly to offer as to the face, which it

P. 91

* ——— the sun, which cometh forth as a bridegroom out of his chamber, and rejoiceth as a giant to run his course. Psalm xix. 5.

† The accounts given in relation to this statue make it so highly probable that it was the great Apollo of Delphos, that, for my own part, I make no manner of doubt of its being so.

will be proper to defer till we have spoken of *light* and *shade* and *colour*.

As some of the ancient statues have been of such singular use to me, I shall beg leave to conclude this chapter with an observation or two on them in general.

It is allowed by the most skilful in the imitative arts, that though there are many of the remains of antiquity that have great excellencies about them, yet there are not, moderately speaking, above twenty that may be justly called *capital*. There is one reason, nevertheless, besides the blind veneration that generally is paid to antiquity, for holding even many very imperfect pieces in some degree of estimation : I mean that *peculiar taste of elegance* which so visibly runs through them all, down to the most incorrect of their basso-relievos : which *taste*, I am persuaded, my reader will now conceive to have been entirely owing to the perfect knowledge the ancients must have had of the use of the precise serpentine-line.

But this cause of *elegance* not having been since sufficiently understood, no wonder such effects should have appeared mysterious, and have drawn mankind into a sort of religious esteem, and even bigotry, to the works of antiquity.

Nor have there been wanting of artful people who have made good profit of those whose unbounded admiration hath run them into enthusiasm. Nay, there are, I believe, some who still carry on a comfortable trade in such originals as have been so defaced and maimed by time that it would be impossible, without a pair of *double-ground* connoisseur-spectacles, to see whether they have ever been good or bad : they deal also in cooked-up copies, which they are very apt to put off for originals. And whoever dares be bold enough to detect such impositions, finds himself immediately branded, and given out as one of low ideas, ignorant of the true sublime, self-conceited, envious, &c.

But as there are a great part of mankind that delight most in what they least understand, for aught I know, the emolument may be equal between the *bubbler* and the *bubbled:* at least this seems to have been Butler's opinion :

> Doubtless the pleasure is as great
> In being cheated, as to cheat.

CHAPTER XII.

OF LIGHT AND SHADE,

AND THE MANNER IN WHICH OBJECTS ARE EXPLAINED TO THE EYE BY THEM.

P. 93 ALTHOUGH both this and the next chapter may seem more particularly relative to the art of painting than any of the foregoing, yet, as hitherto, I have endeavoured to be understood by every reader, so here also I shall avoid, as much as the subject will permit, speaking of what would only be well conceived by painters.

There is such a subtile variety in the nature of appearances, that probably we shall not be able to gain much ground by this enquiry, unless we exert and apply the full use of every sense that will convey to us any information concerning them.

So far as we have already gone, the sense of feeling, as well as that of seeing, hath been applied to; so that perhaps a man born blind, may, by his better touch, that is common to those who have their sight, together with the regular process that has been here given of lines, so feel out the nature of forms, as to make a tolerable judgment of what is beautiful to sight.

Here again our other senses must assist us, not-

withstanding in this chapter we shall be more confined to what is communicated to the eye by rays of
light; and though things must now be considered as
appearances only, produced and made out merely by P.
means of *lights, shades,* and *colours*.

By the various circumstances of which every one
knows we have represented on the flat surface of the
looking-glass, pictures equal to the originals reflected by it. The painter too, by proper dispositions of
lights, shades, and colours on his canvass, will raise
the like ideas. Even prints, by means of lights and
shades alone, will perfectly inform the eye of every
shape and distance whatsoever, in which even lines
must be considered as narrow parts of shade, a number of them, drawn or engraved neatly side by side,
called *hatching*, serve as shades in prints, and when
they are artfully managed, are a kind of pleasing
succedaneum to the delicacy of Nature's.

Could mezzotinto prints be wrought as accurately as those with the graver, they would come nearest to Nature, because they are done without strokes
or lines.

I have often thought that a landskip, in the process of this way of representing it, doth a little resem-
ble the first coming on of day. The copper-plate it is
done upon, when the artist first takes it into hand,
is wrought all over with an edged tool, so as to make
it print one even black, like night; and his whole
work after this is merely introducing the lights into
it, which he does by scraping off the rough grain
according to his design, artfully smoothing it most
where light is most required: but as he proceeds in

P.95 burnishing the lights, and clearing up the shades, he is obliged to take off frequent impressions to prove the progress of the work, so that each proof appears like the different times of a foggy morning, till one becomes so finished as to be distinct and clear enough to imitate a day-light piece. I have given this description, because I think the whole operation, in the simplest manner, shews what lights and shades alone will do.

As light must always be supposed, I need only speak of such privations of it as are called shades, or shadows, wherein I shall endeavour to point out and regularly describe a certain order and arrangement in their appearance, in which order we may conceive different kinds of softenings and modulations of the rays of light which are said to fall upon the eye from every object it sees, and to cause those more or less pleasing vibrations of the optic nerves, which serve to inform the mind concerning every different shape or figure that presents itself.

The best light for seeing the shadows of objects truly, is that which comes in at a common-sized window, where the sun doth not shine; I shall therefore speak of their order as seen by this kind of light: and shall take the liberty, in the present and following chapter, to consider colours but as variegated shades, which, together with common shades, will now be divided into two general parts or branches.

P. 96 The first we shall call PRIME TINTS, by which is meant any colour or colours on the surfaces of objects; and the use we shall make of these different hues will be to consider them as shades to one another. Thus gold is a shade to silver, &c. exclusive of those additional shades which may be made in any degree by the privation of light.

The second branch may be called RETIRING SHADES, which gradate, or go off by degrees, as fig.* These shades, as they vary more or less, produce beauty, whether they are occasioned by the privation of light, or made by the pencilings of art or nature.

When I come to treat of colouring, I shall particularly shew in what manner the gradating of prime tints serve to the making a beautiful complexion; in this place we shall only observe how nature hath by these gradating shades ornamented the surfaces of animals; fish generally have this kind of shade from their backs downward; birds have their feathers enriched with it; and many flowers, particularly the rose, shew it by the gradually increasing colours of their leaves.

The sky always gradates one way or other; and the rising or setting sun exhibits it in great perfection, the imitating of which was Claud. de Lorain's peculiar excellence, and is now Mr Lambert's: there is so much of what is called harmony to the eye to be produced by this shade, that I believe we may venture to say, in art it is the painter's gamut, which nature has sweetly pointed out to us in what we call P. 97 the eyes of a peacock's tail: and the nicest needle-workers are taught to weave it into every flower and leaf, right or wrong, as if it was as constantly to be observed as it is seen in flames of fire; because it is always found to entertain the eye. There is a sort of

* Fig. 34. T. p. 2.

needle-work called Irish-stitch, done in these shades only, which pleases still, though it has long been out of fashion.

There is so strict an analogy between shade and sound, that they may well serve to illustrate each other's qualities : for as sounds gradually decreasing and increasing give the idea of progression from, or to the ear, just so do retiring shades shew progression, by figuring it to the eye. Thus, as by objects growing still fainter, we judge of distances in prospects, so by the decreasing noise of thunder we form the idea of its moving further from us. And, with regard to their similitude in beauty, like as the gradating shade pleases the eye, so the increasing, or swelling note, delights the ear.

I have called it the retiring shade, because by the successive, or continual change in its appearance, it is equally instrumental with converging lines,' in shewing how much objects, or any parts of them, retire or recede from the eye ; without which a floor, or horizontal-plane, would often seem to stand upright P. 98 like a wall. And notwithstanding all the other ways by which we learn to know at what distances things are from us, frequent deceptions happen to the eye on account of deficiencies in this shade : for if the light chances to be so disposed on objects as not to give this shade its true gradating appearance, not only spaces are confounded, but round things appear flat, and flat ones round.

* See p. 7. The two converging lines from the ship to the point C, under fig. 47, plate I.

But although the retiring shade hath this property, when seen with converging lines, yet if it describes no particular form, as none of those do in fig. 94, on top of plate 2, it can only appear as a flat penciled shade; but being inclosed within some known boundary, or outline, such as may signify a wall, a road, a globe, or any other form in perspective where the parts retire, it will then shew its retiring quality : as, for example, the retiring shade on the floor, in plate 2, which gradates from the dog's feet to those of the dancer's, shews, that by this means a level appearance is given to the ground : so when a cube is put into true perspective on paper, with lines only, which do but barely hint the directions every face of it is meant to take, these shades make them seem to retire just as the perspective lines direct, thus mutually completing the idea of those recessions which neither of them alone could do.

Moreover, the outline of a globe is but a circle on the paper; yet, according to the manner of filling up the space within it with this shade, it may be made to appear either flat, globular, or concave, in P. any of its positions with the eye; and as each manner of filling up the circle for those purposes must be very different, it evidently shews the necessity of distinguishing this shade into as many species or kinds as there are classes or species of lines, with which they may have a correspondence.

In doing which it will be found, that by their correspondency with, and conformity to objects, either composed of straight, curved, waving, or serpentine lines, they of course take such appearances of variety as are adequate to the variety made by those lines ; and by this conformity of shades we have the same ideas of any of the objects composed of the above lines in their front aspects, as we have of them by their profiles, which otherwise could not be without feeling them.

Now instead of giving engraved examples of each species of shade, as I have done of lines, I have found that they may be more satisfactorily pointed out and described by having recourse to the life.

But in order to the better and more precisely fixing upon what may be there seen, as the distinct species, of which all the shades of the retiring kind in nature partake, in some degree or other, the following scheme is offered, and intended as an additional means of making such simple impressions in the mind as may be thought adequate to the four species of lines described in Chapter 27. Wherein we are to suppose imperceptible degrees of shade 100 gradating from one figure to another. The first species to be represented by 1, 2, 3, 4, 5.

the second by 5, 4, 3, 2, 1, 2, 3, 4, 5.

and the third by 5, 4, 3, 2, 1, 2, 3, 4, 5, 4, 3, 2, 1, 2, 3, 4, 5. gradating from the dots underneath, repeated either way.

As the first species varies or gradates but one way, it is therefore least ornamental, and equal only to straight lines.

The second gradating contrary ways, doubling the other's variety, is consequently twice as pleasing, and thereby equal to curved lines.

The third species gradating doubly contrary ways,

is thereby still more pleasing in proportion to that
quadruple variety which makes it become capable
of conveying to the mind an equivalent in shade,
which expresses the beauty of the waving line
when it cannot be seen as a line.

The retiring shade, adequate to the serpentine
line, now should follow; but as the line itself could
not be expressed on paper without the figure of a
cone *, so neither can this shade be described without the assistance of a proper form, and therefore
must be deferred a little longer.

When only the ornamental quality of shades is
spoken of, for the sake of distinguishing them from
retiring shades, let them be considered as pencilings
only; whence another advantage will arise, which
is, that then all the intervening mixtures, with their P. 101
degrees of beauty between each species, may be as
easily conceived as those have been between each
class of lines.

And now let us have recourse to the experiments
in life, for such examples as may explain the retiring
power of each species, since, as has been before observed, they must be considered together with their
proper forms, or else their properties cannot be well
distinguished.

All the degrees of obliquity that planes, or flat
surfaces, are capable of moving into, have their appearances of recession perfected by the first species
of retiring shades, which may evidently be seen by

* See Fig. 26. p. I.

setting opposite a door, as it is opening outwards from the eye, and fronting one light.

But it will be proper to premise, that when it is quite shut, and flat or parallel to the eye and window, it will only have a penciling shade gradating upon it, and spreading all around from the middle, but which will not have the power of giving the idea of recession any way, as when it opens and the lines run in perspective to a point; because the square figure or parallel lines of the door do not correspond with such shade; but let a door be circular in the same situation, and all without side, or round about it, painted of any other colour, to make its figure more distinctly seen, and it will immediately appear concave like a bason, the shade continually retiring; P.102 because this circular species of shade would then be accompanied by its corresponding form, a circle *.

But to return: We observed that all the degrees of obliquity in the moving of planes or flat surfaces have the appearances of their recession perfected to the eye by the first species of retiring shade. For example, then, when the door opens, and goes from its parallel situation with the eye, the shade last spoken of may be observed to alter and change its round gradating appearance into that of gradating one way only; as when a standing water takes a current upon the least power given it to descend.

* Note—If the light were to come in at a very little hole not far from the door, so as to make the gradation sudden and strong, like what may be made with a small candle held near a wall or a wainscot, the bason would appear the deeper for it.

Note—If the light should come in at the door-way, instead of the window, the gradation then would be reversed, but still the effect of recession would be just the same, as this shade ever complies with the perspective lines.

In the next place, let us observe the *ovolo*, or quarter-round in a cornice, fronting the eye in like manner, by which may be seen an example of the second species, where, on its most projecting part, a line of light is seen, from whence these shades retire contrary ways, by which the curvature is understood.

And, perhaps, in the very same cornice may be seen an example of the third species, in that ornamental member called by the architects *cyma recta*, or talon, which indeed is no more than a larger sort of waving or ogee moulding, wherein, by the convex parts gently gliding into the concave, you may see four contrasted gradating shades showing so many varied recessions from the eye, by which we are made as sensible of its waving form as if we saw the profile outline of some corner of it, where it is mitred, as the joiners term it. Note—When these objects have a little gloss on them these appearances are most distinct.

Lastly, the serpentine shade may be seen (light and situation as before) by the help of the following

Note also—That when planes are seen parallel to the eye in open day-light, they have scarce any round gradating or penciling shade at all, but appear merely as uniform prime tints, because the rays of light are equally diffused upon them. Nevertheless, give them but obliquity, they will more or less exhibit the retiring shade.

P. 103

figure, as thus—Imagine the horn, fig. 57, plate 2,
to be of so soft a nature, that, with the fingers only,
it might be pressed into any shape, then, beginning
gently from the middle of the dotted line, but pressing harder and harder all the way up the lesser end,
by such pressure there would be as much concave
above as would remain convex below, which would
bring it equal in variety or beauty to the ogee
moulding; but after this, by giving the whole a
twist, like figure 58, these shades must unavoidably
change their appearances, and, in some measure,
twist about as the concave and convex parts are
twisted, and consequently thereby add that variety
P.104 which, of course, will give this species of shade as
much the preference to the foregoing, as forms composed of serpentine lines have to those composed
only of the waving. See Chap. IX. and Chap. X.

I should not have given my reader the trouble of
completing, by the help of his imagination, the foregoing figure, but as it may contribute to the more
ready and particular conception of that intricate variety which twisted figures give to this species of
shade, and to facilitate his understanding the cause
of its beauty, wherever it may be seen on surfaces
of ornament, when it will be found nowhere more
conspicuous than in a fine face, as will be seen upon
further enquiry.

The dotted line *, which begins from the concave
part under the arch of the brow near the nose, and
from thence winding down by the corner of the eye,
and there turning obliquely with the round of the

* Fig. 97. B. p. 1.

cheek, shows the course of that twist of shades in a
face which was before described by the horn, and
which may be most perfectly seen in the life, or in
a marble busto, together with the following additional circumstances still remaining to be described.

As a face is for the most part round, it is therefore apt to receive reflected light on its shadowy
side[1], which not only adds more beauty by another
pleasing tender gradation, but also serves to distin- P.
guish the roundness of the cheeks, &c. from such
parts as sink and fall in ; because concavities do not
admit of reflections as convex forms do[2].

I have now only to add, that, as before observed,
Chap. IV. p. 23, that the oval hath a noble simplicity in it, more equal to its variety than any other object in nature, and of which the general form of a
face is composed ; therefore, from what has been now
shewn, the general gradation-shade belonging to it
must consequently be adequate thereto, and which
evidently gives a delicate softness to the whole composition of a face, insomuch that every little dent,
crack, or scratch the form receives, its shadows also

---

[1] Note—Though I have advised the observing objects by a front
light, for the sake of the better distinguishing our four fundamental
species of shades, yet objects in general are more advantageously
and agreeably seen by light coming sideways upon them, and therefore generally chose in paintings, as it gives an additional reflected
softness, not unlike the gentle tone of an echo in music.

[2] As an instance that convex and concave would appear the same,
if the former were to hav. no reflection thrown upon, observe the
ovolo and cavetto, or channel, in a cornice, placed near together,
and seen by a front light, when they will each of them, by turns,
appear either concave or convex, as fancy shall direct.

suffer with it, and help to show the blemish. Even the least roughness interrupts and damages that soft gradating play of shades which fall upon it. Mr Dryden, describing the light and shades of a face, in his epistle to Sir Godfrey Kneller the portrait-painter, seems, by the penetration of his incomparable genius, to have understood that language in the works of nature, which the latter, by means of an exact eye and a strict obeying hand, could only faithfully transcribe, when he says,

106

> Where light to shades descending, plays, not strives,
> Dies by degrees, and by degrees revives.

CHAPTER XIII.

OF COMPOSITION

WITH REGARD TO LIGHT, SHADE, AND COLOURS.

UNDER this head I shall attempt shewing what it is that gives the appearance of that hollow or vacant space in which all things move so freely, and in what manner light, shade, and colours mark or point out the distances of one object from another, and occasion an agreeable play upon the eye, called by the painters a fine keeping, and pleasing composition of light and shade. Herein my design is to consider this matter as a performance of Nature *without*, or before the eye; I mean, as if the objects with their shades, &c. were in fact circumstanced as they appear, and as the unskilled in optics take them to be. And let it be remarked throughout this chapter, that the pleasure arising from composition, as in a fine landskip, &c. is chiefly owing to the dispositions and assemblages of light and shades, which are so ordered by the principles called OPPOSITION, BREADTH, and SIMPLICITY, as to produce a just and distinct perception of the objects before us.

Experience teaches us that the eye may be subdued and forced into forming and disposing of objects even quite contrary to what it would naturally see

P.107 them, by the prejudgment of the mind from the better authority of feeling, or some other persuasive motive. But surely this extraordinary perversion of the sight would not have been suffered, did it not tend to great and necessary purposes, in rectifying some deficiencies which it would otherwise be subject to (though we must own at the same time, that the mind itself may be so imposed upon as to make the eye see falsely as well as truly); for example, were it not for this controul over the sight, it is well known that we should not only see things double, but upside down, as they are painted upon the retina, and as each eye has a distinct sight. And then as to distances; a fly upon a pane of glass is sometimes imagined a crow, or larger bird afar off, till some circumstance hath rectified the mistake, and convinced us of its real size and place.

Hence I would infer, that the eye generally gives its assent to such space and distances as have been first measured by the feeling, or otherwise calculated in the mind; which measurements and calculations are equally, if not more, in the power of a blind man, as was fully experienced by that incomparable mathematician and wonder of his age, the late professor Sanderson.

By pursuing this observation on the faculties of the mind, an idea may be formed of the means by which we attain to the perception or appearance of an immense space surrounding us; which cavity, being subject to divisions and subdivisions in the mind, is P.108 afterwards fashioned by the limited power of the eye, first into a hemisphere, and then into the appearance of different distances, which are pictured to it by means of such dispositions of light and shade as shall next be described. And these I now desire may be looked upon but as so many *marks*, or *types*, set upon these distances, and which are remembered and learnt by degrees, and, when learnt, are recurred to upon all occasions.

If permitted then to consider light and shades as *types of distinction*, they become, as it were, our materials, of which *prime tints* are the principal ; by these I mean the fixed and permanent colours of each object, as the green of trees, &c. which serve the purposes of separating and relieving the several objects by the different strengths or shades of them being opposed to each other*.

The other shades that have been before spoken of serve and help to the like purposes when properly opposed ; but as in nature they are continually fleeting and changing their appearances, either by our or their situations, they sometimes oppose and relieve, and sometimes not, as for instance ; I once observed the tower-part of a steeple so exactly the colour of a light cloud behind it, that, at the distance I stood, there was not the least distinction to be made, so that the spire (of a lead colour) seemed suspended in the air ; but had a cloud of the like tint with the steeple supplied the place of the white one, the tower would then have been relieved and distinct, when P. the spire would have been lost to the view.

* Fig. 86. T. p. 2.

H

Nor is it sufficient that objects are of different colours, or shades, to shew their distances from the eye, if one does not in part hide, or lay over the other, as in fig. 86.

For as fig. *, the two equal balls, though one were black and the other white, placed on the separate walls, supposed distance from each other twenty or thirty feet, nevertheless may seem both to rest upon one, if the tops of the walls are level with the eye; but when one ball hides part of the other, as in the same figure, we begin to apprehend they are upon different walls, which is determined by the perspective:[1] hence you will see the reason why the steeple of Bloomsbury-church, in coming from Hampstead, seems to stand upon Montague-house, though it is several hundred yards distant from it.

Since then the opposition of one prime tint or shade to another hath so great a share in marking out the recessions, or distances in a prospect, by which the eye is led onward step by step, it becomes a principle of consequence enough to be further discussed, with regard to the management of it in compositions of nature as well as art. As to the management of it, when seen only from one point, the artist hath the advantage over nature, because such fixed dispositions of shades as he hath artfully put together

P. 110

* Fig. 90. T. p. 2.

[1] The knowledge of perspective is no small help to the seeing objects truly, for which purpose Dr Brook Taylor's Linear Perspective, made easy to those who are unacquainted with geometry, may be of most service.

cannot be displaced by the alteration of light, for which reason designs done in two prime tints only, will sufficiently represent all those recessions, and give a just keeping to the representation of a prospect, in a print; whereas the oppositions in nature, depending, as has been before hinted, on accidental situations and uncertain incidents, do not always make such pleasing composition, and would therefore have been very often deficient had Nature worked in two colours only; for which reason she hath provided an infinite number of materials, not only by way of prevention, but to add lustre and beauty to her works.

By an infinite number of materials, I mean colours and shades of all kinds and degrees; some notion of which variety may be formed by supposing a piece of white silk, by several dippings gradually dyed to a black, and carrying it in like manner through the prime tints of yellow, red, and blue; and then again, by making the like progress through all the mixtures that are to be made of these three original colours. So that when we survey this infinite and immense variety, it is no wonder, that, let the light or objects be situated or changed how they will, oppositions seldom miss: nor that even every incident of shade should sometimes be so completely disposed as to admit of no further beauty as to composition; and from P.III whence the artist hath by observation taken his principles of imitation, as in the following respect.

Those objects which are intended most to affect the eye, and come forwardest to the view, must have large, strong, and smart oppositions, like the fore-ground in fig. *, and what are designed to be thrown further off, must be made still weaker and weaker, as expressed in figures 86, 92, and 93, which, receding in order, make a kind of gradation of oppositions, to which, and all the other circumstances already described both for recession and beauty, nature hath added what is known by the name of aerial perspective; being that interposition of air which throws a general soft retiring tint over the whole prospect, to be seen in excess at the rising of a fog. All which again receives still more distinctness, as well as a greater degree of variety, when the sun shines bright, and casts broad shadows of one object upon another; which gives the skilful designer such hints for shewing broad and fine oppositions of shades, as give life and spirit to his performances.

BREADTH OF SHADE is a principle that assists in making distinction more conspicuous; thus fig. †, is better distinguished by its breadth, or quantity of shade, and viewed with more ease and pleasure at any distance than fig. ‡, which hath many, and these but narrow shades between the folds. And for one of the noblest instances of this, let Windsor-castle be viewed at the rising or setting of the sun.

112 Let breadth be introduced how it will, it always gives great repose to the eye; as, on the contrary, when lights and shades in a composition are scattered about in little spots, the eye is constantly disturbed, and the mind is uneasy, especially if you are

* Fig. 89. T. p. 2.   † Fig. 87. L. p. 1.   ‡ Fig. 88. L. p. 1.

eager to understand every object in the composition, as it is painful to the ear when any one is anxious to know what is said in company, where many are talking at the same time.

SIMPLICITY (which I am last to speak of) in the disposition of a great variety, is best accomplished by following Nature's constant rule, of dividing composition into three or five parts, or parcels, see chap. 4. on Simplicity : the painters accordingly divide theirs into fore-ground, middle-ground, and distance, or back-ground; which simple and distinct quantities *mass* together that variety which entertains the eye ; as the different parts of base, tenor, and treble, in a composition of music, entertain the ear.

Let these principles be reversed, or neglected, the light and shade will appear as disagreeable as fig.* ; whereas, was this to be a composition of lights and shades only, properly disposed, though ranged under no particular figures, it might still have the pleasing effect of a picture. And here, as it would be endless to enter upon the different effects of lights and shades on lucid and transparent bodies, we shall leave them to the reader's observation, and so conclude this chapter.

* Fig. 91. T. p. 2.

CHAPTER XIV.

OF COLOURING.

By the beauty of colouring, the painters mean that disposition of colours on objects, together with their proper shades, which appear at the same time both distinctly varied and artfully united in compositions of any kind ; but, by way of pre-eminence, it is generally understood of flesh-colour, when no other composition is named.

To avoid confusion, and having already said enough of retiring shades, I shall now only describe the nature and effect of the prime tint of flesh ; for the composition of this, when rightly understood, comprehends every thing that can be said of the colouring of all other objects whatever.

And herein (as has been shewn in chap. 8, of the manner of composing pleasing forms) the whole process will depend upon the art of varying ; *i. e.* upon an artful manner of varying every colour belonging to flesh, under the direction of the six fundamental principles there spoken of.

But before we proceed to shew in what manner these principles conduce to this design, we shall take a view of Nature's curious ways of producing all sorts

6

of complexions, which may help to further our conception of the principles of varying colours, so as to see why they cause the effect of beauty.

1. It is well known, the fair young girl, the brown P. old man, and the negro; nay, all mankind, have the same appearance, and are alike disagreeable to the eye when the upper skin is taken away; now to conceal so disagreeable an object, and to produce that variety of complexions seen in the world, Nature hath contrived a transparent skin called the cuticula, with a lining to it of a very extraordinary kind, called the cutis; both which are so thin any little scald will make them blister and peel off. These adhering skins are more or less transparent in some parts of the body than in others, and likewise different in different persons. The cuticula alone is like gold-beaters' skin, a little wet, but somewhat thinner, especially in fair young people, which would shew the fat, lean, and all the blood vessels, just as they lie under it, as through isinglass, were it not for its lining the cutis, which is so curiously constructed as to exhibit those things beneath it which are necessary to life and motion, in pleasing arrangements and dispositions of beauty.

The cutis is composed of tender threads like network, filled with different coloured juices. The white juice serves to make the very fair complexion—yellow makes the brunette—brownish yellow, the ruddy brown—green yellow, the olive—dark brown, the mulatto—black, the negro. These different coloured juices, together with the different *meshes* of the net-work, and the size of its threads in this or that part, causes the variety of complexions.

P.115 A description of this manner of its shewing the rosy colour of the cheek, and, in like manner, the bluish tints about the temple, &c. see in the profile *, where you are to suppose the black strokes of the print to be the white threads of the network, and where the strokes are thickest and the part blackest, you are to suppose the flesh would be whitest; so that the lighter part of it stands for the vermilion-colour of the cheek, gradating every way.

Some persons have the net-work so equally wove over the whole body, face and all, that the greatest heat or cold will hardly make them change their colour; and these are seldom seen to blush, though ever so bashful, whilst the texture is so fine in some young women, that they redden or turn pale on the least occasion.

I am apt to think the texture of this net-work is of a very tender kind, subject to damage many ways, but able to recover itself again, especially in youth. The fair fat healthy child of three or four years old hath it in great perfection, most visible when it is moderately warm, but till that age somewhat imperfect.

It is in this manner, then, that Nature seems to do her work.—And now let us see how by art the like appearance may be made and penciled on the surface of an uniform-coloured statue of wax or marble; by describing which operation we shall still more particularly point out what is to our present purpose: I mean the reason why the order Nature hath thus
P.116 made use of should strike us with the idea of beau-

* Fig. 95. T. p. 2.

ty, which, by the way, perhaps may be of more use to some painters than they will care to own.

There are but three original colours in painting besides black and white, viz. red, yellow, and blue. Green and purple are compounded, the first of blue and yellow, the latter of red and blue; however, these compounds being so distinctly different from the original colours, we will rank them as such. Fig. * represents, mixt up as on a painter's pallet, scales of these five original colours divided into seven classes, 1, 2, 3, 4, 5, 6, 7.——4 is the medium and most brilliant class, being that which will appear a firm red, when those of 5, 6, 7 would deviate into white, and those of 1, 2, 3 would sink into black, either by twilight, or at a moderate distance from the eye, which shews 4 to be brightest, and a more permanent colour than the rest. But as white is nearest to light, it may be said to be equal if not superior in value as to beauty with class 4; therefore the classes 5, 6, 7 have also almost equal beauty with it too, because what they lose of their brilliancy and permanency of colour they gain from the white or light; whereas 3, 2, 1 absolutely lose their beauty by degrees as they approach nearer to black, the representative of darkness.

Let us then, for distinction and pre-eminence sake, call class 4 of each colour *bloom tints*, or, if you please, virgin tints, as the painters call them; and once more recollect, that in the disposition of colours as well as of forms, variety, simplicity, distinctness, intrica- P.

* Fig. 94. T. p. 2.

cy, uniformity, and quantity, direct in giving beauty to the colouring of the human frame, especially if we include the face, where uniformity and strong opposition of tints are required, as in the eyes and mouth, which call most for our attention. But for the general hue of flesh now to be described, variety, intricacy, and simplicity are chiefly required.

The value of the degrees of colour being thus considered and ranged in order upon the pallet, fig. 94, let us next apply them to a busto, fig. *, of white marble, which may be supposed to let every tint sink into it, like as a drop of ink sinks in and spreads itself upon coarse paper, whereby each tint will gradate all around.

If you would have the neck of the busto tinged of a very florid and lively complexion, the pencil must be dipt in the bloom tints of each colour as they stand one above another at No. 4.—if for a less florid, in those of No. 5.—if for a very fair, from No. 6; and so on till the marble would scarce be tinged at all : Let therefore No. 6 be our present choice, and begin with penciling on the red, as at r, the yellow tint at y, the blue tint at b, and the purple or lake tint at p.

These four tints thus laid on, proceed to covering the whole neck and breast, but still changing and varying the situations of the tints with one another, also causing their shapes and sizes to differ as much as possible; red must be oftenest repeated, yellow next often, purple red next, and blue but seldom, except in particular parts, as the temples, backs of

P.118

* Fig. 96. R. p. 2.

the hands, &c. where the larger veins show their branching shapes (sometimes too distinctly) still varying those appearances. But there are, no doubt, infinite variations in nature from what may be called the most beautiful order and disposition of the colours in flesh, not only in different persons, but in different parts of the same, all subject to the same principles in some degree or other.

Now, if we imagine this whole process to be made with the tender tints of class 7, as they are supposed to stand, red, yellow, blue, green, and purple, underneath each other, the general hue of the performance will be a seeming uniform prime tint, at any little distance, that is, a very fair, transparent, and pearl-like complexion; but never quite uniform, as snow, ivory, marble, or wax, like a poet's mistress, P. 119 for either of these in living flesh would in truth be hideous.

As in nature, by the general yellowish hue of the cuticula, the gradating of one colour into another appears to be more delicately softened and united together, so will the colours we are supposed to have been laying upon the busto appear to be more united and mellowed by the oils they are ground in, which takes a yellowish cast after a little time, but is apt to do more mischief hereby than good; for which reason care is taken to procure such oil as is clearest, and will best keep its colour[1] in oil-painting.

[1] Notwithstanding the deep-rooted notion, even amongst the majority of painters themselves, that time is a great improver of good pictures, I will undertake to show that nothing can be more absurd. Having mentioned above the whole effect of the oil, let us now see

Upon the whole of this account we find, that the utmost beauty of colouring depends on the great prin-

in what manner time operates on the colours themselves, in order to discover if any changes in them can give a picture more union and harmony than has been in the power of a skilful master, with all his rules of art, to do. When colours change at all it must be somewhat in the manner following, for, as they are made some of metal, some of earth, some of stone, and others of more perishable materials, time cannot operate on them otherwise than as by daily experience we find it doth, which is, that one changes darker, another lighter, one quite to a different colour, whilst another, as ultramarine, will keep its natural brightness even in the fire. Therefore how is it possible that such different materials, ever variously changing, (visibly after a certain time,) should accidentally coincide with the artist's intention, and bring about the greater harmony of the piece, when it is manifestly contrary to their nature; for do we not see, in most collections, that much time disunites, untunes, blackens, and by degrees destroys even the best preserved pictures?

But if, for argument sake, we suppose, that the colours were to fall equally together, let us see what advantage this would give to any sort of composition. We will begin with a flower-piece :——When a master hath painted a rose, a lily, an african, a gentianella, or violet, with his best art and brightest colours, how far short do they fall of the freshness and rich brilliancy of Nature; and shall we wish to see them fall still lower, more faint, sullied, and dirtied by the hand of Time, and then admire them as having gained an additional beauty, and call them mended and heightened, rather than fouled, and in a manner destroyed? how absurd! instead of mellow and softened, therefore, always read yellow and sullied, for this is doing Time the destroyer but common justice. Or shall we desire to see complexions, which in life are often, literally, as brilliant as the flowers above-mentioned, served in the like ungrateful manner? In a landskip, will the water be more transparent, or the sky shine with a greater lustre, when embrowned and darkened by decay? surely no. I own it would be a pity that Mr Addison's beautiful description of Time at work in ciple of varying by all the means of varying, and on the proper and artful union of that variety ; which

the gallery of pictures, and the following lines of Mr Dryden, should want a sufficient foundation :

> For Time shall with his ready pencil stand,
> Retouch your figures with his ripening hand ;
> Mellow your colours, and embrown the tint ;
> Add every grace which time alone can grant ;
> To future ages shall your fame convey,
> And give more beauties than he takes away.
>
> *Dryden to Kneller.*

were it not that the error they are built upon hath been a continual blight to the growth of the art, by misguiding both the proficient and the encourager ; and often compelling the former, contrary to his judgment, to imitate the damaged hue of decayed pictures, so that when his works undergo the like injuries, they must have a double remove from nature, which puts it in the power of the meanest observer to see his deficiencies. Whence another absurd notion hath taken rise, viz. that the colours now-a-days do not stand so well as formerly ; whereas colours well prepared, in which there is but little art or expence, have, and will always have, the same properties in every age, and, without accidents, as damps, bad varnish, and the like, (being laid separate and pure,) will stand and keep together for many years, in defiance of time itself.

In proof of this, let any one take a view of the ceiling at Greenwich-hospital, painted by Sir James Thornhill, forty years ago, which still remains fresh, strong, and clear, as if it had been finished but yesterday: and although several French writers have so learnedly and philosophically proved, that the air of this island is too thick, or——too something, for the genius of a painter, yet France in all her palaces can hardly boast of a nobler, more judicious, or richer performance of its kind. Note——The upper end of the hall, where the royal family is painted, was left chiefly to the pencil of Mr Andrea, a foreigner, after the payment originally agreed upon for the work was so much reduced as made it not worth Sir James's while to finish the whole with his own more masterly hand.

P.120 may be farther proved by supposing the rules here laid down, all or any part of them reversed.

I am apt to believe, that the not knowing Nature's artful and intricate method of uniting colours for the production of the variegated composition, or prime tint of flesh, hath made colouring, in the art of painting, a kind of mystery in all ages; insomuch that it may fairly be said, out of the many thousands who have laboured to attain it, not above ten or P.121 twelve painters have happily succeeded therein. Corregio (who lived in a country-village, and had nothing but the life to study after) is said almost to have stood alone for this particular excellence. Guido, who made beauty his chief aim, was always at a loss about it. Poussin scarce ever obtained a glimpse of it, as is manifest by his many different attempts: indeed France hath not produced one remarkable good colourist.[*]

P.122 Rubens boldly, and in a masterly manner, kept his bloom tints bright, separate, and distinct, but sometimes too much so for easel or cabinet pictures; however, his manner was admirably well calculated for

---

[*] The lame excuse writers on painting have made for the many great masters that have failed in this particular, is, that they purposely deadened their colours, and kept them what they affectedly called *chaste*, that the correctness of their outlines might be seen to greater advantage. Whereas colours cannot be too brilliant, if properly disposed, because the distinction of the parts are thereby made more perfect; as may be seen by comparing a marble busto with the variegated colours of the face either in the life, or one well painted: it is true, uncomposed variety, either in the features or the limbs, as being daubed with many, or one colour, will so confound the parts as to render them unintelligible.

great works, to be seen at a considerable distance, such as his celebrated ceiling at Whitehall-chapel [1]; which, upon a nearer view, will illustrate what I have advanced with regard to the separate brightness of the tints, and show, what indeed is known to every painter, that, had the colours there seen so bright and separate been all smoothed, and absolutely blended together, they would have produced a dirty grey instead of flesh-colour. The difficulty then lies in bringing *blue*, the third original colour, into flesh, on account of the vast variety introduced thereby; and this omitted, all the difficulty ceases; and a common sign-painter, that lays his colours smooth, instantly becomes, in point of colouring, a Rubens, a Titian, or a Corregio.

[1] The front of this building by Inigo Jones, is an additional exemplification of the principles for varying the parts in building; (explained by the candlesticks, &c. chap. VIII.) which would appear to be a stronger proof still, were a building formed of squares on squares; with squares uniformly cut in each square to be opposed to it, to show the reverse.

CHAPTER XV.

OF THE FACE.

HAVING thus spoken briefly of light, shade, and colour, we now return to our lineal account of form,
P.123 as proposed (p. 91.), with regard to the face. It is
an observation, that, out of the great number of
faces that have been formed since the creation of
the world, no two have been so exactly alike, but
that the usual and common discernment of the eye
would discover a difference between them : therefore it is not unreasonable to suppose, that this discernment is still capable of further improvements
by instructions from a methodical enquiry, which
the ingenious Mr Richardson, in his Treatise on
Painting, terms *the art of seeing.*

1. I shall begin with a description of such lines
as compose the features of a face of the highest
taste, and the reverse. See fig. *, taken from an
antique head, which stands in the first rank of estimation : in proof of this, Raphael Urbin, and other
great painters and sculptors, have imitated it for the
characters of their heroes and other great men ; and
the old man's head, fig. †, was modelled in clay by
Fiamingo (and not inferior in its taste of lines to the
best antique,) for the use of Andrea Sacchi, after

* Fig. 97. B. p. 1.   † Fig. 98. L. p. 1.

which model he painted all the heads in his famous
picture of St Romoaldo's Dream; and this picture
hath the reputation of being one of the best pictures in the world [1].

These examples are here chosen to exemplify and
confirm the force of serpentine lines in a face; and
let it also be observed, that, in these master-pieces P.
of art, all the parts are otherwise consistent with
the rules heretofore laid down: I shall therefore
only shew the effects and use of the line of beauty.
One way of proving in what manner the serpentine
line appears to operate in this respect, may be by
pressing several pieces of wire close up and down
the different parts of the face and features of those
casts; which wires will all come off so many serpentine lines, as is partly marked in fig. 97, B. p. 1,
by the dotted lines. The beard and hair of the
head, fig. 98, being a set of loose lines naturally,
and therefore disposable at the painter's or sculptor's pleasure, are remarkably composed in this head
of nothing else but a varied play of serpentine lines
twisting together in a flame-like manner.

But as imperfections are easier to be imitated than
perfections, we shall now have it in our power to explain the latter more fully, by showing the reverse
in several degrees, down to the most contemptible
meanness that lines can be formed into.

Figure 99 is the first degree of deviation from

[1] Note—I must refer the reader to the casts of both these pieces
of sculpture, which are to be found in the hands of the curious, because it is impossible to express all that I intend, with sufficient accuracy, in a print of this size, whatever pains might have been taken
with it, or indeed in any print were it ever so large.

figure 97, where the lines are made straighter, and reduced in quantity; deviating still more in figure 100, more yet in figure 101, and yet more visibly in 102; figure 103 still more so; figure 104 is totally divested of all lines of elegance, like a barber's block; and 105 is composed merely of such plain lines as children make, when of themselves they begin to 125 imitate in drawing a human face. It is evident the inimitable Butler was sensible of the mean and ridiculous effect of such kind of lines, by the description he gives of the shape of Hudibras's beard, fig. *,

> In cut and dye so like a tile,
> A sudden view it would beguile.

9. With regard to character and expression: We have daily many instances which confirm the common received opinion, that the face is the index of the mind; and this maxim is so rooted in us, we can scarce help (if our attention is a little raised) forming some particular conception of the person's mind whose face we are observing, even before we receive information by any other means. How often is it said, on the slightest view, that such a one looks like a good-natured man, that he hath an honest open countenance, or looks like a cunning rogue, a man of sense, or a fool, &c. And how are our eyes rivetted to the aspects of kings and heroes, murderers and saints; and as we contemplate their deeds, seldom fail of making application to their looks. It is reasonable to believe that aspect to be a true and legi-

* Fig. 106. L. p. 1.

ble representation of the mind, which gives every one the same idea at first sight, and is afterwards confirmed in fact : for instance, all concur in the same opinion, at first sight, of a downright idiot.

There is but little to be seen by children's faces, more than that they are heavy or lively ; and scarcely that unless they are in motion. Very handsome faces of almost any age will hide a foolish or a wicked **P.126** mind till they betray themselves by their actions or their words : yet the frequent awkward movements of the muscles of the fool's face, though ever so handsome, is apt in time to leave such traces up and down it as will distinguish a defect of mind upon examination : but the bad man, if he be an hypocrite, may so manage his muscles, by teaching them to contradict his heart, that little of his mind can be gathered from his countenance ; so that the character of an hypocrite is entirely out of the power of the pencil, without some adjoining circumstance to discover him, as smiling and stabbing at the same time, or the like.

It is by the natural and unaffected movements of the muscles, caused by the passions of the mind, that every man's character would in some measure be written in his face by that time he arrives at forty years of age, were it not for certain accidents which often, though not always, prevent it. For the ill-natured man, by frequently frowning, and pouting out the muscles of his mouth, doth in time bring those parts to a constant state of the appearance of ill-nature, which might have been prevented by the constant affectation of a smile ; and so of the other passions : though there are some that do not affect the muscles at all simply of themselves, as love and hope.

But lest I should be thought to lay too great a stress on outward show, like a physiognomist, take this with you, that it is acknowledged there are so many different causes which produce the same kind of movements and appearances of the features, and so many thwartings by accidental shapes in the make of faces, that the old adage, *fronti nulla fides*, will ever stand its ground upon the whole ; and for very wise reasons Nature hath thought fit it should. But, on the other hand, as in many particular cases we receive information from the expressions of the countenance, what follows is meant to give a lineal description of the language written therein.

It may not be amiss just to look over the passions of the mind, from tranquillity to extreme despair, as they are in order described in the common drawing-book, called Le Brun's Passions of the Mind, selected from that great master's works for the use of learners, where you may have a compendious view of all the common expressions at once. And although these are but imperfect copies, they will answer our purpose in this place better than any other thing I can refer you to ; because the passions are there ranged in succession, and distinctly marked with lines only, the shadows being omitted.

Some features are formed so as to make this or that expression of a passion more or less legible ; for example, the little narrow Chinese eye suits a loving or laughing expression best, as a large full eye doth those of fierceness and astonishment; and round-rising muscles will appear with some degree of chearfulness even in sorrow; the features thus suiting with the expressions that have been often P.128 repeated in the face, at length mark it with such lines as sufficiently distinguish the character of the mind.

The ancients in their lowest characters have shewn as much judgment, and as great a degree of taste, in the management and twisting of the lines of them, as in their statues of a sublimer kind; in the former varying only from the precise line of grace in some parts where the character or action required it. The dying gladiator and the dancing fawn, the former a slave, the latter a wild clown, are sculptored in as high a taste of lines as the Antinous or the Apollo, with this difference, that the precise line of grace abounds more in the two last; notwithstanding which it is generally allowed there is equal merit in the former, as there is near as much judgment required for the execution of them. Human nature can hardly be represented more debased than in the character of the Silenus, fig. *, where the bulging-line, fig. 49, No. 7, runs through all the features of the face, as well as the other parts of his swinish body; whereas in the satyr of the wood, though the ancients have joined the brute with the man, we still see preserved an elegant display of serpentine lines, that make it a graceful figure.

Indeed the works of art have need of the whole advantage of this line to make up for its other deficiencies; for though in Nature's works the line of beau-

* Fig. 107. p. 1.

ty is often neglected, or mixed with plain lines, yet so far are they from being defective on this ac-
P.129 count, that by this means there is exhibited that infinite variety of human forms which always distinguishes the hand of Nature from the limited and insufficient one of Art; and as thus she, for the sake of variety upon the whole, deviates sometimes into plain and inelegant lines, if the poor artist is but able now and then to correct and give a better taste to some particular part of what he imitates, by having learnt so to do from her more perfect works, or copying from those that have, ten to one he grows vain upon it, and fancies himself a nature-mender; not considering that even in these, the meanest of her works, she is never wholly destitute of such lines of beauty and other delicacies, as are not only beyond his narrow reach, but are seen wanting even in the most celebrated attempts to rival her. But to return,

As to what we call plain lines, there is this remarkable effect constantly produced by them, that, being more or less conspicuous in any kind of character or expression of the face, they bring along with them certain degrees of a foolish or ridiculous aspect.

It is the inelegance of these lines, which more properly belonging to inanimate bodies, and being seen where lines of more beauty and taste are expected, that renders the face silly and ridiculous. See chap. VI. p. 31.

Children in infancy have movements in the muscles of their faces peculiar to their age, as an uninformed and unmeaning stare, an open mouth, and simple grin: all which expressions are chiefly formed

of plain curves, and these movements and expres- P.130
sions idiots are apt to retain ; so that in time they
mark their faces with these uncouth lines ; and when
the lines coincide and agree with the natural forms
of the features, it becomes a more apparent and confirmed character of an idiot. These plain shapes last
mentioned sometimes happen to people of the best
sense, to some when the features are at rest, to
others when they are put into motion; which a variety of constant regular movements, proceeding
from a good understanding, and fashioned by a
genteel education, will often by degrees correct into lines of more elegance.

That particular expression likewise of the face, or
movement of a feature, which becomes one person,
shall be disagreeable in another, just as such expressions or turns chance to fall in with lines of beauty,
or the reverse ; for this reason there are pretty frowns
and disagreeable smiles: the lines that form a pleasing
smile about the corners of the mouth have gentle
windings, as fig. *, but lose their beauty in the full
laugh, as fig. †. The expression of excessive laughter,
oftener than any other, gives a sensible face a silly or
disagreeable look, as it is apt to form regular plain
lines about the mouth, like a parenthesis, which sometimes appears like crying; as, on the contrary, I remember to have seen a beggar who had clouted up
his head very artfully, and whose visage was thin
and pale enough to excite pity, but his features were
otherwise so unfortunately formed for his purpose, P.131

* Fig. 108. L. p. 2.   † Fig. 109. L. p. 2.

that what he intended for a grin of pain and misery, was rather a joyous laugh.

It is strange that Nature hath afforded us so many lines and shapes to indicate the deficiencies and blemishes of the mind, whilst there are none at all that point out the perfections of it beyond the appearance of common sense and placidity. Deportment, words, and actions, must speak the good, the wise, the witty, the humane, the generous, the merciful, and the brave. Nor are gravity and solemn looks always signs of wisdom : the mind much occupied with trifles will occasion as grave and sagacious an aspect as if it was charged with matters of the utmost moment; the balance-master's attention to a single point, in order to preserve his balance, may look as wise at that time as the greatest philosopher in the depth of his studies. All that the ancient sculptors could do, notwithstanding their enthusiastic endeavours to raise the characters of their deities to aspects of sagacity above human, was to give them features of beauty. Their god of wisdom hath no more in his look than a handsome manliness ; the Jupiter is carried somewhat higher, by giving it a little more severity than the Apollo, by a larger prominency of brow gently bending in seeming thoughtfulness, with an ample beard, which, being added to the noble quantity of its other lines, invests that capital piece of sculpture with uncommon dignity, which, in the mysterious language of a profound connoisseur, is styled a divine idea, inconceivably great, and above nature.

3dly and lastly, I shall shew in what manner the

lines of the face alter from infancy upwards, and specify the different ages. We are now to pay most attention to *simplicity*, as the difference of ages we are about to speak of turn chiefly upon the use made of this principle, in a greater or less degree, in the form of the lines.

From infancy till the body has done growing, the contents both of the body and the face, and every part of their surface, are daily changing into more variety, till they obtain a certain medium, (see page 78 on proportion,) from which medium, as fig. *, if we return back to infancy, we shall see the variety decreasing, till by degrees that simplicity in the form which gave variety its due limits, deviates into sameness; so that all the parts of the face may be circumscribed in several circles, as fig. †.

But there is another very extraordinary circumstance (perhaps never taken notice of before in this light) which nature hath given us to distinguish one age from another by; which is, that though every feature grows larger and longer, till the whole person has done growing, the sight of the eye still keeps its original size; I mean the pupil, with its iris, or ring, for the diameter of this circle continues still the same, and so becomes a fixed measure by which we, as it were, insensibly compare the daily perceived growings of the other parts of the face, and thereby determine a young person's age. You may sometimes find this part of the eye in a new-born infant **p.**

* Fig. 113. B. p. 2.   † Fig. 116. L. p. 2.

full as large as in a man of six foot; nay, sometimes larger, see fig. *, and †.

In infancy the faces of boys and girls have no visible difference ‡; but as they grow up, the features of the boy get the start, and grow faster in proportion to the ring of the eye than those of the girl, which shews the distinction of the sex in the face. Boys who have larger features than ordinary, in proportion to the rings of their eyes, are what we call manly-featured children; as those who have the contrary, look more childish and younger than they really are. It is this proportion of the features with the eyes that makes women, when they are dressed in men's clothes, look so young and boyish: but as Nature doth not always stick close to these particulars, we may be mistaken both in sexes and ages.

By these obvious appearances, and the differences of the whole size, we easily judge of ages till twenty, but not with such certainty afterwards; for the alterations from that age are of a different kind, subject to other changes by growing fatter or leaner,

* Fig. 110. B. p. 2.   † Fig. 114. B. p. 2.
‡ Fig. 115. T. p. 1. which represents three different sizes of the pupil of the eye; the least was exactly taken from the eye of a large-featured man, aged 105; the biggest from one of twenty, who had this part larger than ordinary, and the other is the common size. If this part of the eye in the pictures of Charles II. and James II. painted by Vandyke at Kensington, were to be measured with a pair of compasses, and compared with their pictures, painted by Lilly, when they were men, the diameters would be found in both pictures respectively the same.

which, it is well known, often give a different turn to the look of the person with regard to his age.

The hair of the head, which encompasses a face as a frame doth a picture, and contrasts with its uniform colour the variegated inclosed composition, adding more or less beauty thereto according as it is disposed by the rules of art, is another indication of advanced age.

What remains to be said on the different appear- P. 134 ances of ages, being less pleasing than what has gone before, shall be described with more brevity. In the age from twenty to thirty, barring accidents, there appears but little change, either in the colours or the lines of the face; for though the bloom tints may go off a little, yet, on the other hand, the make of the features often attain a sort of settled firmness in them, aided by an air of acquired sensibility, which makes ample amends for that loss, and keeps beauty till thirty pretty much upon a par; after this time, as the alterations grow more and more visible, we perceive the sweet simplicity of many rounding parts of the face begin to break into dented shapes, with more sudden turns about the muscles, occasioned by their many repeated movements; as also by dividing the broad parts, and thereby taking off the large sweeps of the serpentine lines; the shades of beauty also consequently suffering in their softnesses. Something of what is here meant between the two ages of thirty and fifty, see in figures*, and

* Fig. 117. and Fig. 118. B. p. 2.

what further havock Time continues to make after the age of fifty is too remarkable to need describing : the strokes and cuts he then lays on are plain enough ; however, in spite of all his malice, those lineaments that have once been elegant retain their flowing turns in venerable age, leaving to the last a comely piece of ruins.

CHAPTER XVI.

OF ATTITUDE.

P. 135 Such dispositions of the body and limbs as appear most graceful when seen at rest, depend upon gentle winding contrasts, mostly governed by the precise serpentine line, which, in attitudes of authority, are more extended and spreading than ordinary, but reduced somewhat below the medium of grace in those of negligence and ease : and as much exaggerated in insolent and proud carriage, or in distortions of pain, (see figure 9, plate 1.) as lessened and contracted into plain and parallel lines, to express meanness, awkwardness, and submission.

The general idea of an action, as well as of an attitude, may be given with a pencil in very few lines. It is easy to conceive that the attitude of a person upon the cross, may be fully signified by the two straight lines of the cross ; so the extended manner of St Andrew's crucifixion is wholly understood by the X-like cross.

Thus, as two or three lines at first are sufficient to shew the intention of an attitude, I will take this opportunity of presenting my reader (who may have been at the trouble of following me thus far) with the sketch of a country-dance, in the manner I began to set out the design, in order to shew how few lines are necessary to express the first thoughts, as P. 136

to different attitudes; see fig *, which describe, in some measure, the several figures and actions, mostly of the ridiculous kind, that are represented in the chief part of plate 2.

The most amiable person may deform his general appearance by throwing his body and limbs into plain lines; but such lines appear still in a more disagreeable light in people of a particular make; I have therefore chose such figures as I thought would agree best with my first score of lines, fig. 71.

The two parts of curves next to 71, served for the figures of the old woman and her partner at the farther end of the room. The curve and two straight lines at right angles, gave the hint for the fat man's sprawling posture. I next resolved to keep a figure within the bounds of a circle, which produced the upper part of the fat woman, between the fat man and the awkward one in the bag-wig, for whom I had made a sort of an X. The prim lady, his partner, in the riding-habit, by pecking back her elbows, as they call it, from the waist upwards, made a tolerable D, with a straight line under it, to signify the scanty stiffness of her petticoat; and a Z stood for the angular position the body makes with the legs and thighs of the affected fellow in the tye-wig; the upper parts of his plump partner was confined to an O, and this changed into a P, served as a hint for the straight lines behind. The uniform diamond of P. 137 a card was filled up by the flying dress, &c. of the little capering figure in the spencer-wig; whilst a double L marked the parallel position of his poking

* Fig. 71. T. p. 2.

partner's hands and arms: and, lastly, the two waving lines were drawn for the more genteel turns of the two figures at the hither end.

The best representation in a picture, of even the most elegant dancing, as every figure is rather a suspended action in it than an attitude, must be always somewhat unnatural and ridiculous; for were it possible, in a real dance, to fix every person at one instant of time, as in a picture, not one in twenty would appear to be graceful, though each were ever so much so in their movements; nor could the figure of the dance itself be at all understood.

The dancing-room is also ornamented purposely with such statues and pictures as may serve to a farther illustration. Henry the Eighth, fig. *, makes a perfect X with his legs and arms; and the position of Charles the First, fig. †, is composed of less varied lines than the statue of Edward the Sixth, fig. ‡, and the medal over his head is in the like kind of lines; but that over Q. Elizabeth, as well as her figure, is in the contrary; so are also the two other wooden figures at the end. Likewise the comical posture of astonishment, (expressed by following the direction of one plain curve, as the dotted line in a French print of Sancho, where Don Quixote demolishes the puppet-shew, fig. §,) is a good contrast to the effect of the serpentine lines in the fine turn of the Samaritan woman, fig. ‖, taken from one of the best pictures Annibal Carrache ever painted. P.

* Fig. 72. p. 2.   † Fig. 51. p. 2.   ‡ Fig. 73. p. 2.
§ Fig. 75. R. p. 2.   ‖ Fig. 74. L. p. 2.

CHAPTER XVII.

OF ACTION.

To the amazing variety of forms made still infinitely more various in appearance by light, shade, and colour, Nature hath added another way of increasing that variety, still more to enhance the value of all her compositions. This is accomplished by means of action, the fullest display of which is put into the power of the human species, and which is equally subject to the same principles with regard to the effects of beauty, or the reverse, as govern all the former compositions; as is partly seen in chapter XI. on Proportion. My business here shall be, in as concise a manner as possible, to particularise the application of these principles to the movement of the body, and therewith finish this *system* of variety in forms and actions.

There is no one but would wish to have it in his power to be genteel and graceful in the carriage of his person, could it be attained with little trouble and expence of time. The usual methods relied on for this purpose among well-bred people, take up a considerable part of their time: nay, even those of the first rank have no other recourse in these matters than to dancing-masters and fencing-masters: dan-
139 cing and fencing are undoubtedly proper, and very

necessary accomplishments; yet are they frequently very imperfect in bringing about the business of graceful deportment. For although the muscles of the body may attain a pliancy by these exercises, and the limbs, by the elegant movement in dancing, acquire a facility in moving gracefully, yet for want of knowing the meaning of every grace, and whereon it depends, affectations and misapplications often follow.

Action is a sort of language which perhaps one time or other may come to be taught by a kind of grammar-rules; but, at present, is only got by rote and imitation; and, contrary to most other copyings or imitations, people of rank and fortune generally excel their originals, the dancing-masters, in easy behaviour and unaffected grace; as a sense of superiority makes them act without constraint, especially when their persons are well-turned. If so, what can be more conducive to that freedom and necessary courage which make acquired grace seem easy and natural, than the being able to demonstrate *when* we are actually just and proper in the least movement we perform; whereas, for want of such certainty in the mind, if one of the most finished gentlemen at court was to appear as an actor on the public stage, he would find himself at a loss how to move properly, and be stiff, narrow, and awkward in representing even his own character: the uncertainty of being right would naturally give him some of that restraint which the uneducated common people generally have P. when they appear before their betters.

It is known that bodies in motion always describe some line or other in the air, as the whirling round of a fire-brand apparently makes a circle, the water-fall part of a curve, the arrow and bullet, by the swiftness of their motions, nearly a straight line; waving lines are formed by the pleasing movement of a ship on the waves. Now, in order to obtain a just idea of action, at the same time to be judiciously satisfied of being in the right in what we do, let us begin with imagining a line formed in the air by any supposed point at the end of a limb or part that is moved, or made by the whole part, or limb; or by the whole body together. And that thus much of movements may be conceived at once is evident on the least recollection; for whoever has seen a fine Arabian war-horse, unbacked and at liberty, and in a wanton trot, cannot but remember what a large waving line his rising, and at the same time pressing forward, cuts through the air; the equal continuation of which is varied by his curveting from side to side; whilst his long mane and tail play about in serpentine movements.

After thus having formed the idea of all movements being as lines, it will not be difficult to conceive, that grace in action depends upon the same principles as have been shewn to produce it in forms.

The next thing that offers itself to our consideration is the force of *habit* and custom in action, for a great deal depends thereon.

141 The peculiar movements of each person, as the gait in walking, are particularised in such lines as each part describes by the habits they have contracted. The nature and power of habit may be fully conceived by the following familiar instance, as the mo-

2

tions of one part of the body may serve to explain those of the whole.

Observe, that whatever habit the fingers get in the use of the pen, you see exactly delineated to the eye by the shapes of the letters. Were the movements of every writer's fingers to be precisely the same, one hand-writing would not be known from another; but as the fingers naturally fall into, or acquire different habits of moving, every hand-writing is visibly different. Which movements must tally with the letters, though they are too quick and too small to be as perfectly traced by the eye; but this shews what nice differences are caused, and constantly retained, by habitual movements.

It may be remarked, that all useful habitual motions, such as are readiest to serve the necessary purposes of life, are those made up of plain lines, *i. e.* straight and circular lines, which most animals have in common with mankind, though not in so extensive a degree: the monkey, from his make, hath it sufficiently in his power to be graceful; but as reason is required for this purpose, it would be impossible to bring him to move genteelly.

Though I have said that the ordinary actions of the body are performed in plain lines, I mean only comparatively so with those of studied movements in the serpentine line; for as all our muscles are ever ready to act, when one part is moved, (as an hand or arm, by its proper movers, for raising up or drawing down,) the adjacent muscles act in some degree in correspondence with them: therefore our most common movements are but seldom performed in such

P.142

absolutely mean lines as those of jointed dolls and puppets. A man must have a good deal of practice to be able to mimic such very straight or round motions, which, being incompatible with the human form, are therefore ridiculous.

Let it be observed, that graceful movements in serpentine lines are used but occasionally, and rather at times of leisure, than constantly applied to every action we make. The whole business of life may be carried on without them, they being, properly speaking, only the ornamental part of gesture, and therefore, not being naturally familiarised by necessity, must be acquired by precept or imitation, and reduced to habit by frequent repetitions. *Precept* is the means I should recommend as the most expeditious and effectual way. But before we proceed to the method I have to propose for the more ready and sure way of accustoming the limbs to a facility in the ornamental way of moving, I should observe, that quick time gives it spirit and vivacity, as slow time gravity and solemnity; and further, that the latter of these allows the eye an opportunity of seeing the line of grace to advantage, as in the address of heroes P. 143 on the stage, or in any solemn act of ceremony; and that although time in movement is reduced to certain rules for dancing, it is left more at large and at discretion for deportment.

We come now to offer an odd, but perhaps efficacious method of acquiring a habit of moving in the lines of grace and beauty.

1. Let any one chalk the line fig. *, on a flat sur-

* Fig. 119. L. p. 2.

face, beginning at either end, and he will move his hand and arm in a beautiful direction; but if he chalks the same sort of line on an ogee-moulding of a foot or two in breadth, as the dotted line on figure *, his hand must move in that more beautiful direction which is distinguished by the name of grace ; and according to the quantity given to those lines, great-ness will be added to grace, and the movement will be more or less noble.

Gentle movements of this sort, thus understood, may be made at any time and any where, which, by frequent repetitions, will become so familiar to the parts so exercised, that, on proper occasion, they make them as it were of their own accord.

The pleasing effect of this manner of moving the hand is seen when a snuff-box, or fan, is presented gracefully or genteelly to a lady, both in the hand moving forward and in its return ; but care must be taken that the line of movement be but gentle, as No. 3, fig. 49, plate 1, and not too S-like and twirl-ing, as No. 7 in the same figure : which excess would be affected and ridiculous.

Daily practising these movements with the hands P.144 and arms, as also with such other parts of the body as are capable of them, will, in a short time, render the whole person graceful and easy at pleasure.

2. As to the motions of the *head*, the awe most children are in before strangers, till they come to a certain age, is the cause of their dropping and draw-ing their chins down into their breasts, and looking

* Fig. 120. L. p. 2,

under their foreheads, as if conscious of their weakness, or of something wrong about them. To prevent this awkward shyness, parents and tutors are continually teasing them to hold up their heads, which, if they get them to do, it is with difficulty, and of course in so constrained a manner that it gives the children pain, so that they naturally take all opportunities of easing themselves by holding down their heads, which posture would be full as uneasy to them were it not a relief from restraint : and there is another misfortune in holding down the head, that it is apt to make them bend too much in the back; when this happens to be the case, they then have recourse to steel-collars and other iron machines, all which shacklings are repugnant to nature, and may make the body grow crooked. This daily fatigue, both to the children and the parents, may be avoided, and an ugly habit prevented, by only (at a proper age) fastening a ribbon to a quantity of plaited hair, or to the cap, so as it may be kept fast in its place, and the P. 145 other end to the back of the coat, as fig. *, of such a length as may prevent them drawing their chins into their necks ; which ribbon will always leave the head at liberty to move in any direction but this awkward one they are so apt to fall into.

But till children arrive at a reasoning age, it will be difficult by any means to teach them more grace than what is natural to every well-made child at liberty.

The grace of the upper parts of the body is most

* Fig. 121. L. p. 2.

engaging, and sensible well-made people, in any station, naturally have it in a great degree; therefore rules, unless they are simple and easily retained and practised, are of little use, nay, rather are of disservice.

Holding the head erect is but occasionally right, a proper recline of it may be as graceful; but true elegance is mostly seen in the moving it from one position to another.

And this may be attained by a sensibility within yourself, though you have not a sight of what you do by looking in the glass, when with your head, assisted by a sway of the body in order to give it more scope, you endeavour to make that very serpentine line in the air, which the hands have been before taught to do by the help of the ogee-moulding; and I will venture to say, a few careful repetitions at first setting out will make this movement as easy to the head as to the hands and arms.

The most graceful bow is got by the head's moving in this direction, as it goes downward and rises up again. Some awkward imitators of this elegant way of bowing, for want of knowing what they were P. 146 about, have seemed to bow with wry necks. The low solemn bow to majesty should have but a very little twist, if any, as more becoming gravity and submission. The clownish nod, in a sudden straight line, is quite the reverse of these spoken of.

The most elegant and respectful curtesy hath a gentle, or small degree of the above graceful bowing of the head as the person sinks, and rises, and retreats. If it should be said, that a fine curtesy consists in no more than in being erect in person at the time of sinking and rising, Madam Catherine in clock-work, or the dancing bears led about the street for a show, must be allowed to make as good a curtesy as any body.

N. B. It is necessary in bowing and curtesying to shun an exact sameness at all times; for however graceful it may be on some occasions, at other times it may seem formal and improper. Shakespear seems to have meant the above-spoken-of ornamental manner of bowing, in Enobarbus's description of Cleopatra's waiting-women.———

——— And made their bends adorning.   Act 2.

3. Of *Dancing*. The minuet is allowed by the dancing-masters themselves to be the perfection of all dancing. I once heard an eminent dancing-master say, that the minuet had been the study of his whole life, and that he had been indefatigable in the pursuit of its beauties, yet at last he could only say with Socrates, *he knew nothing:* adding, that I was happy in my profession as a painter, in that some bounds might be set to the study of it. No doubt, as the minuet contains in it a composed variety of as many movements in the serpentine lines as can well be put together in distinct quantities, it is a fine composition of movements.

The ordinary undulating motion of the body in common walking (as may be plainly seen by the waving line, which the shadow a man's head makes against a wall as he is walking between it and the

P.147

afternoon sun) is augmented in dancing into a larger quantity of *waving* by means of the minuet-step, which is so contrived as to raise the body by gentle degrees somewhat higher than ordinary, and sink it again in the same manner lower in the going on of the dance. The figure of the minuet-path on the floor is also composed of serpentine lines, as fig. *, varying a little with the fashion: when the parties, by means of this step, rise and fall most smoothly in time, and free from sudden starting and dropping, they come nearest to Shakespear's idea of the beauty of dancing, in the following lines:

—————————— What you do,
Still betters what is done,—
—When you do dance, I wish you
A wave o' th' sea, that you might ever do
Nothing but that: move still, still so,
And own no other function.—   WINTER's TALE.

The other beauties belonging to this dance are, P. 146 the turns of the head, and twist of the body, in passing each other, as also gentle bowing and presenting hands in the manner before described; all which together displays the greatest variety of movements in serpentine lines imaginable, keeping equal pace with musical time.

There are other dances that entertain merely because they are composed of variety of movements and performed in proper time, but the less they consist of serpentine or waving lines the lower they are

* Fig. 122. T. p. 2.

in the estimation of dancing-masters; for, as has been shown, when the form of the body is divested of its serpentine lines, it becomes ridiculous as a human figure, so likewise when all movements in such lines are excluded in a dance, it becomes low, grotesque, and comical; but however being, as was said, composed of variety, made consistent with some character, and executed with agility, it nevertheless is very entertaining. Such are Italian peasant-dances, &c. But such uncouth contortions of the body as are allowable in a man would disgust in a woman; as the extreme graceful, so very alluring in this sex, is nauseous in the other; even the minuet-grace in a man would hardly be approved, but as the main drift of it represents repeated addresses to the lady.

There is a much greater consistency in the dances of the Italian theatre than of the French, notwithstanding dancing seems to be the genius of that nation; the following distinctly marked characters P.149 were originally from Italy; and, if we consider them lineally as to their particular movements, we shall see wherein their humour consists.

The attitudes of the harlequin are ingeniously composed of certain little quick movements of the head, hands, and feet, some of which shoot out as it were from the body in straight lines, or are twirled about in little circles.

Scaramouch is gravely absurd as the character is intended, in over-stretched tedious movements of unnatural lengths of lines: these two characters seem to have been contrived by conceiving a direct opposition of movements.

Pierrott's movements and attitudes are chiefly in perpendiculars and parallels, so is his figure and dress.

Punchinello is droll by being the reverse of all elegance, both as to movement and figure; the beauty of variety is totally and comically excluded from this character in every respect; his limbs are raised and let fall almost altogether at one time, in parallel directions, as if his seeming fewer joints than ordinary were no better than the hinges of a door.

Dances that represent provincial characters, as these above do, or very low people, such as gardeners, sailors, &c. in merriment, are generally most entertaining on the stage: the Italians have lately added great pleasantry and humour to several French dances, particularly the wooden-shoe dance, in which there is a continual shifting from one attitude in plain lines to another; both the man and the wo- P. 150 man often comically fix themselves in uniform positions, and frequently start, in equal time, into angular forms, one of which remarkably represents two W's in a line, as over figure 122, plate 2. These sort of dances a little raised, especially on the woman's side, in expressing elegant wantonness (which is the true spirit of dancing,) have of late years been most delightfully done, and seem at present to have got the better of pompous, unmeaning, grand ballets; serious dancing being even a contradiction in terms.

4thly. Of *Country Dancing*. The lines which a number of people together form in country or figure dancing, make a delightful play upon the eye, especially when the whole figure is to be seen at one view, as at the play-house from the gallery; the beauty of this kind of mystic dancing, as the poets term it, depends upon moving in a composed variety of lines, chiefly serpentine, governed by the principles of intricacy, &c. The dances of barbarians are always represented without these movements, being only composed of wild skipping, jumping, and turning round, or running backward and forward, with convulsive shrugs and distorted gestures.

One of the most pleasing movements in country dancing, and which answers to all the principles of varying at once, is what they call the hay; the figure of it altogether is a cypher of S's, or a number of serpentine lines interlacing, or intervolving each P.151 other, which suppose traced on the floor, the lines would appear as fig. * Milton in his Paradise Lost, describing the angels dancing about the sacred hill, pictures the whole idea in words:

> Mystical dance !————
> ————Mazes intricate,
> Eccentric, intervolved, yet regular
> Then most, when most irregular they seem.

I shall venture, lastly, to say a word or two of stage-action. From what has been said of habitually moving in waving lines, it may possibly be found that, if stage-action, particularly the graceful, was to be studied lineally, it might be more speedily and

* Fig. 123. T. p. 2.

accurately acquired by the help of the foregoing principles than the methods hitherto taken. It is known that common deportment, such as may pass for elegant and proper off the stage, would no more be thought sufficient upon it than the dialogue of common polite conversation would be accurate or spirited enough for the language of a play. So that trusting to chance only will not do. The actions of every scene ought to be as much as possible a complete composition of well-varied movements, considered as such abstractedly, and apart from what may be merely relative to the sense of the words. Action, considered with regard to assisting the author's meaning, by enforcing the sentiments or raising the passions, must be left entirely to the judgment of the performer; we only pretend to show how the limbs may be made to have an equal readiness to move in all such directions as may be required.

What I would have understood by action, ab- P. stractedly and apart from its giving force to the meaning of the words, may be better conceived by supposing a foreigner, who is a thorough master of all the effects of action at one of our theatres, but quite ignorant of the language of the play; it is evident his sentiments, under such limitations, would chiefly arise from what he might distinguish by the lines of the movements belonging to each character; the actions of an old man, if proper or not, would be visible to him at once, and he would judge of low and odd characters by the inelegant lines which we have already shown to belong to the characters of Punch, Harlequin, Pierrott, or the Clown; so he would also form his judgment of the graceful acting of a fine gentleman, or hero, by the elegance of their movements in such lines of grace and beauty as have been sufficiently described. See chapters 5, 6, 7, 8, on the composition of forms: where note, that as the whole of beauty depends upon *continually varying,* the same must be observed with regard to genteel and elegant acting; and as plain space makes a considerable part of beauty in form, so cessation of movement in acting is as absolutely necessary, and, in my opinion, much wanted on most stages, to relieve the eye from what Shakespear calls, *continually sawing the air.*

The actress hath sufficient grace with fewer actions, and those in less extended lines than the actor; for, as the lines that compose the Venus are simpler and more gently flowing than those that P.153 compose the Apollo, so must her movements be in like proportion.

And here it may not be improper to take notice of a mischief that attends copied actions on the stage; they are often confined to certain sets and numbers, which being repeated, and growing stale to the audience, become at last subject to mimickry and ridicule, which would hardly be the case if an actor were possessed of such general principles as include a knowledge of the effects of all the movements that the body is capable of.

The comedian, whose business it is to imitate the actions belonging to particular characters in nature, may also find his account in the knowledge of lines; for whatever he copies from thelife, by these principles may be strengthened, altered, and adjusted as his judgment shall direct, and the part the author has given him shall require.

FINIS.

EDINBURGH:
Printed by James Ballantyne & Co.

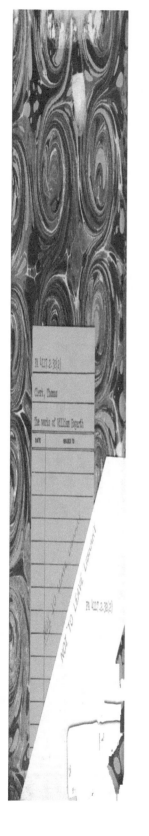

Check Out More Titles From HardPress Classics Series In this collection we are offering thousands of classic and hard to find books. This series spans a vast array of subjects — so you are bound to find something of interest to enjoy reading and learning about.

Subjects:
Architecture
Art
Biography & Autobiography
Body, Mind &Spirit
Children & Young Adult
Dramas
Education
Fiction
History
Language Arts & Disciplines
Law
Literary Collections
Music
Poetry
Psychology
Science
…and many more.

Visit us at www.hardpress.net

Im The Story

personalised classic books

JANE
IN
WONDERLAND

LEWIS
CARROLL

"Beautiful gift... lovely finish.
My Niece loves it, so precious!"

Helen R Brumfieldon

☆☆☆☆☆

UNIQUE GIFT

FOR KIDS, PARTNERS
AND FRIENDS

Timeless books such as:

Kids

Alice in Wonderland · The Jungle Book · The Wonderful Wizard of Oz
Peter and Wendy · Robin Hood · The Prince and The Pauper
The Railway Children · Treasure Island · A Christmas Carol

Adults

Romeo and Juliet · Dracula

Highly
Customizable

Change
Books Title

Replace
Characters Names
with yours

Upload
Photo for
inside page!

Add
Inscriptions

Visit

Im The Story .com

and order yours today!